Nintex Workflow

User's Guide

Learn how to use
Nintex Workflow
in SharePoint and Office 365

Martijn Bleikertz

I would like to dedicate this book
to my two beautiful girls.
Every day I enjoy their smiles, support and help.
Brigitte, Thanks, babe, I love you.

— Martijn

Table of Contents

6 Creating advanced workflows

7 Working with external sources

8 Almost programming

Warning and Disclaimer

Every effort has been made to make this book as complete and as accurate as possible, but no warranty or fitness is implied. The information provided is on an "as is" basis. The author and the publisher shall have neither liability nor responsibility to any person or entity with respect to any loss or damages arising from the information contained in this book or from the use of programs accompanying it. Any errors that have been reported since this book was published are listed on http://bit.ly/18iQfyX

Trademarks

Trademarked names, logos and images may appear in this book. Rather than use a trademark symbol with every occurrence of a trademarked name, logo or image we use the names, logos, and images only in an editorial fashion and to the benefit of the trademark owner, with no intention of infringement of the trademark.
The use in this publication of trade names, trademarks, service marks, and similar terms, even if they are not identified as such, is not to be taken as an expression of opinion as to whether or not they are subject to proprietary rights.
SharePoint, Office365, Excel Service, SQL, Windows are registered trademarks of Microsoft Corporation. Nintex, Nintex Workflow and Nintex Workflow for Office 365 are registered trademark of Nintex.
All other trademarks are the property of their respective owners.

Copyright

About the Author

Martijn Bleikertz is the owner of BleiCon and has worked for nearly a decade as a consultant for several high technology companies. Since early 2007 Martijn got in contact with SharePoint and from that moment on worked almost exclusive on SharePoint projects.

To automate processes and lower the learning curve for people that started to work with SharePoint, Martijn used workflows and was really excited about the products like Nintex Workflow has to offer for not only end-users but also for it-pro's.

Martijn provides training and hands-on courses for customers as they can develop and maintain their own workflows. He is also available for developing custom workflows.

1 • Introduction

Welcome to this book dedicated to the use of Nintex Workflow. We wanted to create this book as a reference for students of our trainings and because we think that Nintex Workflow is one of the best SharePoint workflow solutions out there. If your company is researching the use of workflows in your SharePoint environment to automate processes and help end users they sure have to look at Nintex Workflows.

Audience

This book is for those who want to explore the functionality of Nintex Workflow, people that are orientating on the use of Nintex Workflows, those who are starting to work with Nintex Workflow or users that use it as reference in their day to day job. Our audience during trainings varies from department managers that approve workflows, information workers that want to automate processes and developers that want to solve issues with Nintex Workflow. With these users in mind we have created this book.

As Nintex Workflow is installed on SharePoint and the creation of workflows goes via the SharePoint interface we assume that you have a basic knowledge of SharePoint. You know what sites are, what a library and a list are and how to work with documents and items in these libraries and lists.

This book includes several hands-on assignments to help you get familiar with the use of Nintex Workflow. We encourage you to do these hands-on steps in a development environment. Creating a development environment or configuring the service applications for these hands-on can be complex and may require the help from an IT-Pro.

The book is organized into the following sections:

- **Introduction**, that's this chapter. We explain the requirements for the hands-on and the advanced hands-on exercises
- **Introduction to Nintex Workflow.** In this section we introduce you to what a workflow is, what SharePoint and Nintex Workflow are and see what all the fuss is about
- **Setup and Administration.** This section takes you through the steps of setting up Nintex and configuring in your SharePoint environment. We discuss the upgrade steps if you're coming from a lower version of SharePoint and Nintex. The installation of Nintex Live will be explained
- **The Workflow Designer.** How do you start to create a workflow but also save and manage workflows in Nintex
- **Simple workflows.** We start easy, just a few workflows to get familiarized in working with Nintex Workflow
- **Creating advanced workflows.** In this section we are going to work with variables, constants, conditions and more
- **Workflow with external sources.** Integrate external data from other systems in SharePoint workflows
- **Almost programming.** This section explains what state machine workflows are and how you can use them
- **Other functions.** There are a lot of options as reporting and exclusions that can help you when creating and managing workflows, these options are explained in this section
- **Maintaining Nintex Workflow.** Working with Nintex Workflow on a day to day job
- **Where to go from here.** What do you need to know more when you are creating workflows
- **Actions.** An overview of the most important actions there are.

What you will need

As stated this book will have several hands-on assignments of working with Nintex Workflow that require a SharePoint environment. There are three ways by which you can do these hands-on exercises: you could use an Office 365 environment, you can use a demo environment from Nintex or you could use a local environment.

When you have chosen for an Office 365 or an environment hosted at Nintex you can't carry out the hands-on assignments in chapter **Setup and Administration** as Nintex Workflow on Office 365 and the Nintex environment don't require an installation.

For the local environment we have chosen to use a SharePoint 2010 environment to create this book, as most organizations are on the moment of creation still on SharePoint 2010. The difference in functionality between the Nintex Workflow versions depend on the version. If you're working with SharePoint 2013 and Nintex Workflow 2013 you can find your way through this book as the structure of SharePoint 2010 and 2013 are close to each other. The difference between SharePoint 2007 and SharePoint 2010 is bigger and we advise you to look at upgrading to a newer version if possible.

If you want to do these hands-on exercises, and we strongly recommend you to do these as we believe you learn more by hands-on experience than by theory you need to follow the hardware and software requirements for the SharePoint 2010 environment.

Hardware requirements

For the creation of this book we have used 2 SharePoint environments, one environment where all functions are installed on one server and an environment where Active Directory, the databases and SharePoint are separated over 3 servers.

The first environment is good for practices and development purposes but not supported by Microsoft for production. The second environment is used for practices that are close to a real production environment. In the second scenario we also used different service account for SQL and the SharePoint services as best practices from Microsoft conducts.

Here are the hardware requirements for the environments:
- Single server with Active Directory, SQL and SharePoint installed all in one.
    - Virtual machine with 8192MB and 4 CPU cores
- Three server farm with an Active Directory Domain controller, an SQL 2008 server and a SharePoint 2010 server.
    - 3 Virtual machines Domain Controller with 512MB and 1 CPU core, SQL 2008 with 6GB and 4 CPU cores and SharePoint with 4096MB and 4 CPU cores

The environment you choose doesn't have an impact on the hands-on exercises, these can be made on the single server or three server farm. As you might expect the first environment will perform slower than the second.

Software requirements

Operating system

Nintex is installed on the same servers where SharePoint is installed, therefore the specification for the operating system are equal to that of SharePoint requirements, 64-bit Microsoft Windows Server 2008 or 2008 R2.

Browser support

The browser requirements are Microsoft Internet Explorer 7.x although Microsoft Internet Explorer 8 or greater is recommended. The newer versions of Google Chrome and Firefox are also supported.

SharePoint

In this book we use SharePoint Server 2010 Enterprise, Nintex Workflows 2010 can be installed on any version of SharePoint: Foundation, Standard or Enterprise. Nintex Workflow knows on which version it is installed and disables actions that are not available in that version. Some hands-on practices may require InfoPath that is only available in SharePoint 2010 Enterprise and therefore we use that SharePoint version.

Database server

For the installation of SharePoint installation the following SQL server versions are supported by SharePoint 2010:

- The 64-bit edition of Microsoft SQL Server 2012.
- The 64-bit edition of Microsoft SQL Server 2008 R2.
- The 64-bit edition of Microsoft SQL Server 2008 with Service Pack 1 (SP1) and Cumulative Update 2.
- The 64-bit edition of Microsoft SQL Server 2005 with Service Pack 3 (SP3).

The Nintex query database action can work with any database that uses the OLEDB and ODBC generic connections, for more information about this action see the section **Working with External sources.**

Nintex software

If you have not already downloaded Nintex Workflow you can download a trial version from the Nintex website listed on the next page. The trial will be for the enterprise version of Nintex, so you will get to test all the features, including the hands-on exercises that require enterprise features.

Later on we are going into the licensing details from Nintex.
The trail license will be sent to the e-mail address you provided during the sing-up and is active for 30 days from the day you request it. Our advice is therefore to download the software and trail license when you are ready to test it.

SharePoint installation

We are not going into the details of installing and configuring a SharePoint environment, if you need information about that you can find a lot of good articles online or ask your IT service provider. You require, at minimum, an own site collection. An own farm is very helpful during the **Setup and Administration** chapter of this book.

In this book we want to show you as much as possible of the functionality that's available in Nintex Workflow and have therefore configured the following SharePoint services:
* Business Data Connectivity Service
* Managed Metadata Service
* Search Service
* Secure Store Service
* User Profile Service

Business Data Connectivity Service

To connect to LOB applications we use a Business Data Connectivity Service (BCS Service). In the examples we use the AdventureWorksLT2012 demo database and have this database installed on the SQL server. You can get this database from the following URL http://msftdbprodsamples.codeplex.com.

Search Service

The Search service is configured to crawl the web application where Nintex Workflow is configured. Because the indexing of content is a resource intensive process we don't set an indexing schedule, a manual crawl is used to create the index.

Secure Store Service

The secure Store Service application is used for storing the account that makes a connection to the BCS Service and retrieve the data from the AdventureWorksLT2012 database. The account provided in the Secure Store Service application has data read permissions on that database.

User Profile Service

For the actions **Query user profile** and **Update user profile** we've configured the user profile service application.

2 • Introduction to Nintex Workflow

What is Nintex Workflow?

Nintex Workflow is a product created by Nintex, their started in Australia and are now based in the USA. They have also locations in England, Australia  and Malaysia. Nintex is the world's leading SharePoint workflow company, they are even the number one add on for SharePoint with over 5000 customers in 90 countries reaching 7 million users. These customers are serviced by a global network of high quality partners and service providers.

Nintex customers are government, public, and private organizations including over 200 of the Fortune 500, and over 100 major banks. From simple workflows, to complex processes that interconnect multiple systems, Nintex is revolutionizing the way organizations automate business processes.

Nintex has also other SharePoint solutions as Nintex Reporting, Nintex Analytics and the also very popular Nintex Forms. With Nintex Forms you can easily create forms for most common devices.

Nintex Workflow is a software solution created for building workflows in SharePoint and built on Windows Workflow Foundation. OK, that's nice, but first what is a workflow, and what is SharePoint?

What's a Workflow?
If you look at the definition of a workflow from Wikipedia it is described as:

A workflow consists of a sequence of connected steps where each step follows without delay or gap and ends just before the subsequent step may begin. It is a depiction of a sequence of operations, declared as work of a person or group, an organization of staff, or one or more simple or complex mechanisms. Workflow may be seen as any abstraction of real work.

So a workflow is a sequence of steps following each other and that may be seen as real work. You see that Wikipedia doesn't say that these steps are automated, it just refers to them as a sequence of operations. A secretary that collects signatures for an approval process is therefor a valid workflow.

In this book we are going to try to automate these manual workflows into digital workflows so we can make them more manageable and predictable.

When talking about automation there are two types of automation possible: fully automated workflows that run by themselves and where no user interaction is required, and half automated workflows where a user starts or provides input to the workflow. Most of the workflows in this book are going to be half automated where some sort of user interaction is required, but there are sections that can be used to create fully automated workflows.

Workflow management is used when we are talking about the management of workflows within your organisation via a software application. Because Nintex Workflow has workflow management functions integrated in the product we are going to look at these option in feature sections.

What's SharePoint?

SharePoint is a Web application platform developed by Microsoft and has historically been associated with intranet, content management and document management, by a common technical infrastructure. SharePoint can be used to provide intranet portals, document & file management, collaboration, social networks, extranets, websites, enterprise search and business intelligence. It also has system integration, process integration, and workflow automation capabilities. And that last part is where we in this book are interested in as Nintex Workflow uses this functionality.

One of the most used examples of a workflow in SharePoint is the approval of a document before it's available, this is called the publishing of a document.

Nintex Workflow 2010 can be installed on every version of SharePoint 2010 (foundation, standard or Enterprise) however Nintex features that require Enterprise functionality are not available with Foundation or Standard.

SharePoint Versions

For every SharePoint version there is also a Nintex Workflow version, this book uses the Nintex Workflow 2010 version. Besides this 2010 version they have also created Nintex Workflow 2007 for MOSS 2007 and Workflow 2013 for SharePoint 2013. The version for Office 365 is just called that: Nintex Workflow for Office 365.

Many organizations use SharePoint for Business process management as SharePoint is a flexible, adjustable and powerful system. If you combine this with the use of workflow management you get an even more powerful environment.

Workflow applications

If you want to create workflows in SharePoint you have a few options:
- You stick to the out of the box workflows;
- Create workflows with SharePoint Designer with or without Visio;
- Start using Visual Studio;
- Use a third party application like Nintex Workflow.

Out of the box workflows

SharePoint has a few out of the box workflows that are available after activation of the features. These workflows are approval, approval for deletion and feedback on documents or pages. There is a three stage workflow but the options are very limited.

SharePoint Designer

With SharePoint Designer you can create workflows that do a better job than the out of the box workflows. You can create lookups and by using tricks, you can even create advanced SharePoint Designer workflows.

SharePoint Designer works via a line structured layout, every workflow action is on a separate line that makes managing these workflows daunting.

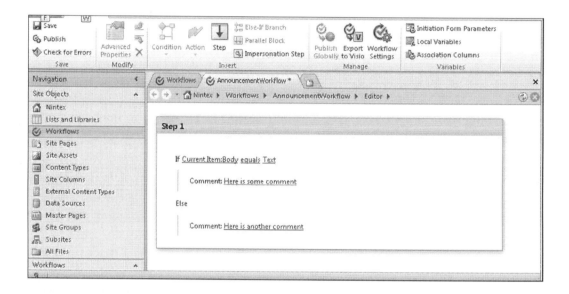

Microsoft Visio

In Microsoft Visio Premium 2010, you can create a workflow in Visio and then export it to Microsoft SharePoint Designer 2010. Business or process analysts who are familiar with flowcharting in Visio can use Visio to design a workflow that represents their business logic, export the workflow, and enable a site owner or IT professional using SharePoint Designer to implement it in SharePoint 2010.

Nice you think, the graphical overview of Visio combined with the workflow functionality of Designer, however there is a catch; Visio Premium is the version of Visio that ticks all the boxes of options and is therefore the most expensive. At the same time after importing the workflow in SharePoint Designer it becomes that same flat structured workflow as with the other designer workflows.

2 • Introduction to Nintex Workflow

Visual studio

Most developers will say "workflows need to be created by Visual Studio, there you have all the control you want!" And if I was a developer I would say the same. But creating workflows with Visual Studio is a complex process and also requires a lot of knowledge of Visual Studio and the SharePoint foundation framework. That's something you don't want to ask from your users.
Modifying a workflow isn't possible without Visual Studio and requires every time a full update of the workflow.

Third party applications

As you have seen in the above sections, creating and maintaining workflows via the standard products in SharePoint isn't that easy. The learning curve to create workflows can be steep for end-users and the flexibly for changes is limited. And that's where applications like Nintex Workflow do a great job in filling this gap; they lower the curve via easy interfaces and use smart variables to provide more flexibility. Some of these applications even adds functions that aren't available in all other applications to deliver a true added value.

Why Nintex Workflow?

So there are other applications available that you can use to create workflows, there are applications that are free, applications that are easy, some are comprehensive others are built in. So why should you use Nintex? Here are a few options that we think make it worth using Nintex workflow.

Visual structure

When designing a workflow it is important to understand the flow and structure of your workflow. Therefore almost all users start their workflows in a program like Visio as they like to view the flow process. Being able to have a logical view is one of the best features of Nintex Workflow and this might even be the reason why users easily adapt to Nintex Workflow in comparison with SharePoint Designer that is a line based workflow designer.

Quick

Creating workflow via the visual drag and drop structure makes creating workflows with Nintex Workflow an easy and quick task. Actions are grouped together in logical sections and can be pre-filled saved. Templates can be used for standard workflows that users can use direct.

Instead of days, workflows are now created in hours.

Workflow history

Besides knowing how your workflow is going to run, it's also important to know how your workflow has run. Why did your workflow set a value? Why did the workflow return an error? This is what you use the workflow history for. Nintex Workflow provides a workflow history that uses a graphic overview of your workflow where with colors the steps that are taken are showed. The green actions are executed, the grey actions are ignored. If your workflow is running your actions are yellow.

Reporting

With the installation of Nintex Workflow you also get web parts that you can use for creating reports. These web parts display information such as: usage summaries, completed vs. error workflow or overdue workflows and can be configured to show this data in chart- or list- views. By adding the chart web part to your reporting pages you can get a quick overview of the status of your Nintex Workflow. There is also a handy web part that shows all running workflows awaiting your approval, perfect for the front-page of a portal!

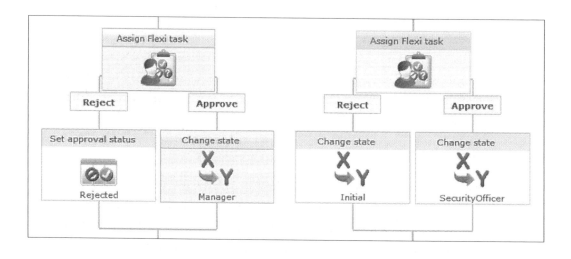

LazyApproval

When you enable LazyApproval you can let your users respond to approval request directly from their e-mail. If a request for approval task is set to a user he almost always receive an e-mail message with a link to the task. After enabling LazyApproval the user only has to reply to the e-mail he receives with approve or deny in the header to approve or deny the task.

Nintex Live

Nintex Live is an online catalog from where you can download actions for use in your Office 365 or local environment. With Nintex Live you can extend your Nintex Workflow application with social features like Twitter, Facebook and LinkedIn. You can also add storage actions like Dropbox, Box or Google Drive, or use the online calculation functions from StrikeIron.
Nintex Live makes it possible to create a hybrid environment where your local SharePoint farm is connected to your Office 365 cloud solutions.

And maybe the best part is that the Nintex Live catalog continues to grow with new actions.

On site and online

The look, feel and functions are almost identical for Nintex Workflow on Office 365 and on site making it for end users easy to adopt to both versions. You could for example use an Office 365 environment with Nintex workflows to let your company collaborate with his partners and a local environment for your internal users only.

Nintex website

The website of Nintex contains a lot of information about Nintex Workflow and other Nintex products. If you want help with an action, more information, examples you can always have a look at http://connect.nintex.com. This is the site of Nintex where you can exchange ideas, tips & tricks.

Nintex versioning

Nintex is continually updating their software, adding new functions and improving exciting functionality to make Nintex Workflow an even better product. If you have selected software assurance with your Nintex purchase you always receive the latest version of Nintex Workflow and you can easily upgrade to a newer version.

Summary

2 • Introduction to Nintex Workflow

In this chapter we have looked at the introduction of Nintex Workflow.
What is SharePoint and what is a workflow in SharePoint?
Which workflow applications are there and how does Nintex compares to these
and we have looked at the advantages of using Nintex Workflow.

One thing to remember:

In the end it isn't about the features that are added,
but is about the value they add.

3 • Setup and Administration

How do you setup Nintex Workflow?

In this chapter, we are going to install and configure Nintex Workflow in your environment. What are the steps that are required for installing the software and how do you configure it?

There is a difference in installing Nintex Workflow for Office 365 environment and installing it on a local farm. When using the Office 365 version you aren't actually installing any software, you are working with the app model of Microsoft SharePoint 2013. If you're installing Nintex Workflow on a local farm you are installing the software directly on the server. We start with the Office 365 setup.

Setup on Office 365

Nintex Workflow for Office 365 is hosted in the cloud using the new SharePoint App model. This means that SharePoint is hosted at a Microsoft datacenter and where Nintex Workflow is running at the datacenter of Nintex. They are maintaining the infrastructure so we can focus on building business processes.

If there isn't a site collection for apps this needs to be created first, any Office 365 administrator can create this.

To add Nintex Workflow as an app go to the SharePoint section of Office 365.

Choose apps from the left navigation and select then Purchase Apps

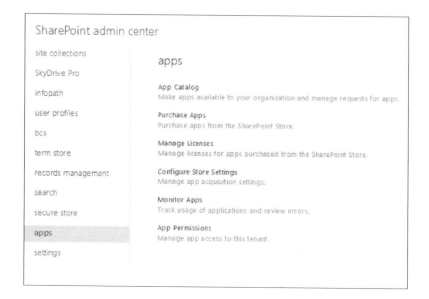

Select Workflow + Process Management from the left navigation and choose Nintex Workflow for Office 365.

3 • Setup and Administration

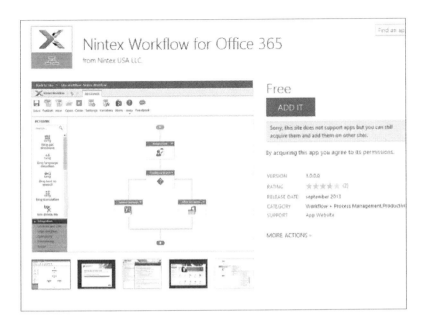

On the Confirmation page click Continue, the app will be added to the app store. Now the App Nintex Workflow for Office 365 is available.

After enabling the Nintex Workflow for Office 365 app the 30 days trial starts or you can enter your subscription Key.

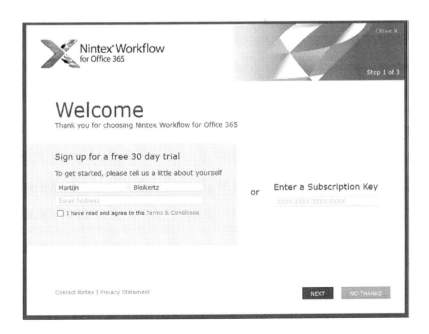

These are the only setups that are required for the setup on Office 365.
One warning the setup on a local farm isn't that easy and fast.

Setup on local farm

We assume that you know how to set up SharePoint or have a SharePoint environment set up for you.

Next, the required steps through the setup, including installing your license and getting ready to author your first workflow will be explained.

Nintex Workflow does not require any client-side software. You need to install Nintex Workflow software on every SharePoint Front-end server that interacts with SharePoint users also known as WFE servers. The best approach is to perform the installation and setup first in a lab environment if this is your first Nintex Workflow Software installation. There are some pitfalls during the installation, so don't risk your production environment.

Before we are going to install Nintex Workflow on an environment it's best to check first if this environment does have the required specifications for running Nintex Workflow. There is nothing worse than having a new shiny application that doesn't perform and therefor not used by users. Here are the requirements.

Hardware Requirements

A question we do receive often from customers is what the hardware requirements are for running Nintex Workflow. There is no exact number to give as it really depends on the use of the SharePoint environment and the usage of workflows in that environment. You can understand that running a farm for 100 users that sometimes start a workflow is something totally different from running a 10K user environment with lots of long running workflows. The best approach is to follow the Microsoft recommended database http://technet.microsoft.com/library/cc678868%28office.14%29.aspx and server guidelines http://technet.microsoft.com/en-us/library/cc850692.aspx

Software requirements

Nintex Workflow can be installed on every SharePoint 2010 version,
it doesn't matter if you choose SharePoint Foundation 2010, SharePoint 2010 Standard or SharePoint 2010 Enterprise.

The actions that require SharePoint 2010 Enterprise aren't available in SharePoint Foundation, it "sees" which version you are using and greys out the actions that aren't available in your SharePoint version.

Permissions

You need to have administrative permissions on the SharePoint server to install Nintex Workflow, this includes farm administrator and create database permissions. Nintex Workflow uses a separate database to store all workflow data including the workflow history.

You should configure your SharePoint environment with incoming and outgoing e-mail settings. Workflow features often rely on e-mail communications to relay task assignments or to allow workflow interaction through incoming e-mail. Users will not always look at a tasks list at their SharePoint site but they do have their e-mail client open during the day and can interact via that.

Installation and deployment

At this point, you should have downloaded the latest version of Nintex Workflow from the Nintex website. Nintex Workflow software is available in different languages, in this book we are using the English version, but you can choose the language you prefer. You can use the Nintex trial license file or use your own license file. Microsoft SQL and SharePoint must be already installed and configured in your environment.

Start the setup by double-clicking the .msi and follow the installation Wizard. You need to accept the license agreement before you can install the software so please read it (like we always do, right?). There are 2 steps during the installation that need some more explanation, these are **add the solution to SharePoint** and Install **Nintex Live**.

The question to add the solutions to SharePoint is asked because automatically adding the solutions will force an IISRESET. When IIS is restarted the site is temporarily un-enviable and needs to rebuild his cache, users can then experience downtime or performance issues.

Installing Nintex Live will install the software and certificates you need to use Nintex Live in your environment. Nintex Live is a Nintex Workflow enterprise feature, if you are not going to use Nintex Workflow enterprise features or don't want Nintex Live you don't have to deploy it. Don't be afraid, selecting the deployment of Nintex Live doesn't enable it for users directly.

After the install wizard is completed, you are automatically directed to the Central Administration site to deploy your solution.

You can also navigate to Central Administration to activate the Nintex Solutions via System settings, Manage farm solutions. You should see the Nintex Solutions there, as shown in the Figure Solution Management. In that figure, we have deployed Nintex Live. Nintex Workflow and Nintex Workflow Enterprise are deployed to the webapplication http://sp2010-1-nintex/

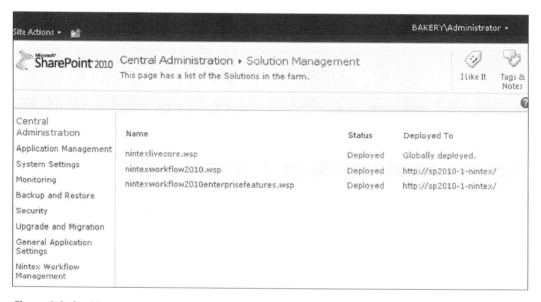

Figure. Solution Management

For each of the Nintex solutions, click the name of the solution, and then click Deploy Solution. Select the web application to which you want to deploy Nintex Workflow, and choose the time for deployment. In a lab/test environment, **All content web applications** and **Now** are allowed. Hit **OK**, and your deployment should be done.

The selected web applications get an application pool recycle and users can receive a temporary unavailability of the site.

Central Administration Setup

Once you have deployed the solution, go to the front-page of Central Administration. You will see 2 new sections called Nintex Workflow Management and Nintex Live Management, as shown below

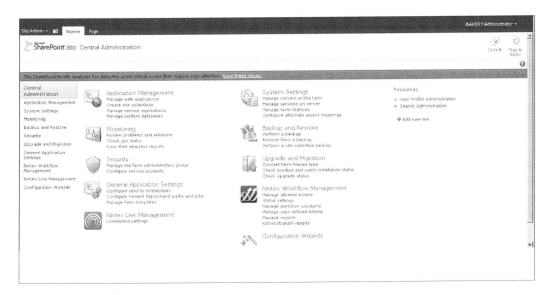

Figure. Nintex workflow management

License

The first step you need to do after the setup is installing the license.
Go to Nintex Workflow Management and click the Licensing link, click Import, browse to the license file you have received from Nintex, and finally hit Import to add your license. Your license page should now display the license details. This is also a nice time to tell you a little bit more about licensing.

Standard, Enterprise or Workgroup

Nintex Workflow licenses are there in three flavors, Standard, Enterprise and Workgroup. What version of Nintex you need depends on what your needs are. Here are in short the biggest difference:

- The Enterprise license contains all available actions where with the Workgroup and Standard license the set of available actions are limited. Almost all the integration actions with other systems are Enterprise feature;
- There is no difference between the set of available actions in the Standard and Workgroup license, only the activation of the software is different;
- Summary statistics, report web parts and chart web parts are Enterprise options
- User-based workflow tracking web parts are for Workgroup and Standard license on site level, with Enterprise license these are on farm level.

The activation difference per license type:

- Per Server – for the Enterprise Edition and Standard Edition a license is required for each SharePoint front-end server where user interaction with Nintex Workflow components occurs;
- Per Site – the Workgroup Edition license covers a single SharePoint front-end server environment with up to five team sites. Only one Workgroup Edition license can be purchased. If more than five site activations or multiple front-end servers are required, a Standard or Enterprise Edition license is required.

So if for example you want to buy Nintex workflow Standard Edition for three severs you need to buy three licenses. In the application form you specify the names of the servers that act as front-end servers. Be aware that the Nintex license is server specific.

> **Nintex licenses are server specific and changing the name of a server results can result in errors.**

Licensing of fail-over servers and cluster based disaster recovery systems is determined according to the number of active instances that can occur simultaneously. For example, an active/passive or cold fail-over configuration does not require a separate license, while active/active or warm/hot fail-over configurations require every instance to be licensed.

Database

Your second step will be to set up the Nintex database. Nintex Workflow uses a separate database to store configuration and workflow content. Go to the database configuration by clicking **Database setup**.

The first time you enter this page, you will have the option to create a new configuration database. Click the **Create** button to do so. You will be asked for the database server, which may be the same server you use for SharePoint databases, as well as the database name.

> **Check if there is a naming convention requirement within your organization for databases.**

If you are using a separate SQL account for database access you can set up that in the last section of the page or just leave the recommended Windows Authentication enabled. Nintex Workflow will create the configuration database when you click **OK** and then take you back to the Database Setup page where you will now see your settings for the configuration database, as shown in Figure Database setup page.

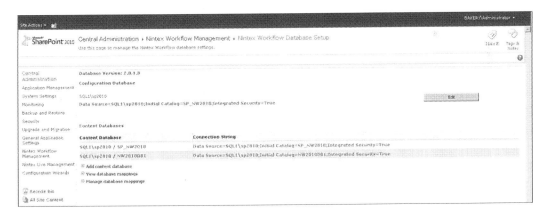

Figure. Database setup page

The third step is to go back to the Application Management page and click **Web Application activation**. This page will allow you to activate Nintex Workflow for a web application or all web applications in a farm. Select the web application for which you want to activate Nintex Workflow, optionally select "All content web applications," and click **Activate**.

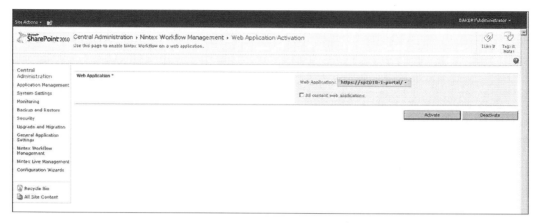

Figure. Activation on Web application

Manage allowed action

The next step in the list is to enable the workflow actions that users are allowed to perform. You can enable or disable workflow actions in the Central Administration per farm or web application. If for example your organization doesn't use Microsoft Dynamics CRM or Lync it's best to not enable these actions to help users from accidentally selecting these actions.

On Site collection level you can also change the allowed actions. If for example you don't want to allow users to configure SQL actions except for the IT pro's you can disable the SQL actions on the user's site collections. The IT pro's can still use the SQL actions on their site collections,

Click on Manage allowed actions to go to that page, and see all the actions that are available within Nintex Workflow Enterprise. Notice that some actions can be disabled/greyed out. You can hover your mouse pointer over a checkbox to see why the action is not allowable. For example, the Query BDC and Query Excel Services actions require that you have SharePoint Enterprise installed.

Global Settings

The last configuration options we are going to look at is the global settings, for the options have a look at the chapter **Additional Options**.

There are 2 important options that need to be configured; the SMTP Server and OCS/Lync.

The SMTP server is by default your default e-mail server, but you could use a different one.
If you want to use the Office Communicator or Lync client actions you also need to configure the Instant messaging settings.

There are a few options in the Global Settings area that may needs to be discussed with IT security:

- Enforce allowed actions at run time; check if the actions are still allowed when the workflow is executed;
- Allow workflow schedules to impersonate the system account; the workflows can be executed as the system account and will have full control;
- Execute SQL action to impersonate the application pool identity; as the app pool account has permissions to the SharePoint databases you could use this account for SQL actions.

More about Global Settings later in the chapter **Additional Options**

Features and Activation

Ok, that's enough configuration for now, let's see some Nintex Workflow in action and check if our setup is configured correctly. Before we can use Nintex Workflow we need to activate it on Site collection and site level.

Go to the site where you want to use Nintex Workflow. On that site, go to the Site Settings page, available from the Site Actions menu. Then, under Site Collection Administration Section select Site Collection Features. You should see four features related to Nintex Workflow, as shown in the Figure Site collection features. Activate the feature called Nintex Workflow 2010. You can leave the other features deactivated for now.

Figure. Site collection features

Activating the Nintex Workflow 2010 site collection feature will prepare the site collection for using Nintex Workflow. Technically, the feature will add a hidden list template, several content types, and some site columns, all used to support the authoring and running of workflows.

You can verify the activation of the site collection feature by clicking the "Site content types" link, the group Nintex Workflow will be created and contain a few content types.
After activating the site collection Nintex Workflow feature, you can return to the Site Settings page and then select the Manage site features page. You will find a feature named Nintex Workflow 2010.

Activate the site feature now.
After the activation return to the Site Settings page where you'll find a new section Nintex Workflow. This is where you will configure Nintex Workflow settings for this site or, in the case of the root web of a site collection, the settings for the site collection. See figure Nintex Workflow settings.

Activation steps:
1. **Activate the Web application in Central admin**
2. **Activate on the Site Collection**
3. **Activate on the Site**

Nintex Workflow
Workflows gallery
Message templates
Workflow templates
Allowed workflow designers
LazyApproval settings
Manage workflow constants
Scheduled workflows
Manage allowed actions
Manage holidays
Workflow change approval
Manage workflow history lists
Manage User Defined Actions
Workflow error notifications
Purge workflow data

Figure. Nintex Workflow settings

Perhaps you have seen it when you clicked on Site Actions, there is a new section in this menu for Nintex Workflow 2010. More information about this menu when we go into details about all the nuts and bolts of Nintex.

Next, go to any list or library in your site. If you have used a standard Team Site template for your site, you can, for example, go to the Shared Documents library. If you have created a blank site or another template without lists, just create any list or library, because you can delete it after testing. Once in the list, click on the Library tab in the top bar and select from the pool down under the Workflow settings the option Create a workflow in Nintex Workflow, as shown in figure 'Workflow settings'.

When you create a new workflow in Nintex Workflow, the first thing that pops up is a dialog box, allowing you to select a template for your new workflow. Nintex Workflow ships with several premade templates from which you can choose, and you can also add your own templates to this collection.

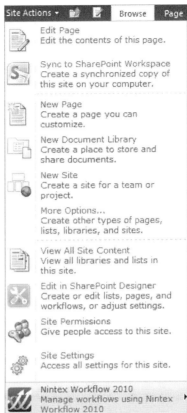

Figure. Nintex Workflow menu

Figure. Workflow settings

Select the Blank template option when you want to create the workflow manually, but consider learning at least which premade templates are available.
The figure on the next page shows the template selection dialog box.

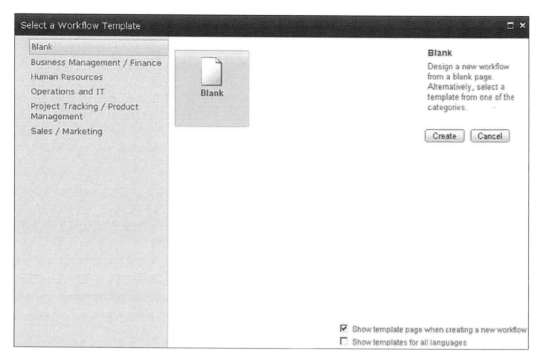

Figure. Template selection dialog box

The pre-made templates are somewhat useful out of the box, but the true benefit comes from modifying the templates. Start with one existing template, and then modify the workflow based on that template. Not only will you save time, but you can take inspiration from the templates and use Nintex Workflow for scenarios you may not have considered already. For example, did you know that you have a pre-made template for employee absence management?

Go to the Human Resources category, and select Absence Manager Approval from the templates. Click the Create button to fill the Workflow Designer window with the premade template, as shown in figure Absence Manager Approval template on the next page.

Upgrade Nintex workflow 2007 to 2010

As customers are migrating from SharePoint 2007 to 2010 or 2013 they also want to migrate their Nintex Workflows to the corresponding edition. Nintex follows the two methods of upgrading supported by Microsoft; the "In Place" upgrade and the "Attach database" upgrade.

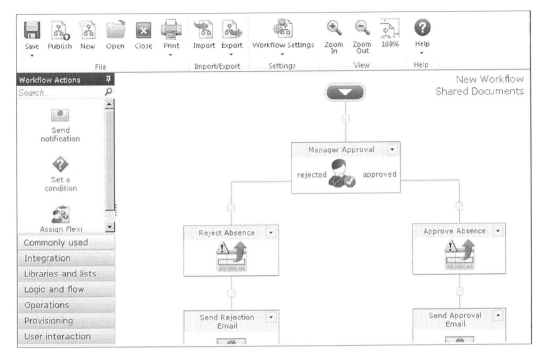

Figure. Absence Manager Approval template

In place upgrade

By an in place upgrade you upgrade your current SharePoint 2007 farm to SharePoint 2010, the SharePoint environment will then continue to run on the same hardware.

First check if your current hardware and software support an in-place upgrade; SharePoint 2010 requires a 64-bit Windows server 2008 SP2 or R2 version where SharePoint 2007 can still run on a Windows 2003 server.

Here are in short the steps you need to follow for an in-place upgrade:
1. You have the SharePoint 2007 environment completely upgraded to SharePoint 2010
2. Uninstall the Nintex workflow 2007 software via the Add remove programs in the control panel
3. Disable the workflow timer service in the Central administration
4. Retract and remove the Nintex workflow 2007 solutions from the SharePoint environment
5. Install the Nintex workflow 2010 software

6. Import the Nintex workflow 2010 license you received from Nintex
7. Browse to the database setup page and select the option "update now option"
8. Enable Nintex Workflow on all the required web applications
9. Enable the Nintex Workflow 2010 workflow actions
10. Perform an IISRESET on all web front end servers in the farm
11. Re-enable Nintex Live if required
12. Enable the workflow timer service back again
13. Create a test workflow and run this, also run an existing workflow.

Attach database upgrade

In the attach databases upgrade scenario SharePoint 2010 is installed on a new farm and the databases need to be moved from the SharePoint 2007 environment to SharePoint 2010. When the databases are attached they are then converted from SharePoint 2007 to SharePoint 2010.

Here are in short the steps you need to follow to do the upgrade:
1. SharePoint 2010 is installed and configured in your new environment
2. The SharePoint 2007 databases are not attached
3. Web application to host the 2007 content is created
4. If you already use Nintex Live in the 2007 environment save the Live ID as you need to reuse it in the SharePoint 2010 farm
5. Disable the workflow timer service in the Central administration
6. Install the Nintex workflow 2010 software
7. Import the Nintex workflow 2010 license you received from Nintex
8. Choose a new database or an existing one
9. Enable the Nintex Workflow 2010 workflow actions
10. Restore the Live ID
11. Attach the SharePoint 2007 databases to the farm
12. Enable Nintex Workflow on all the required web applications
13. Enable the workflow timer service back again
14. Restart the SharePoint timer service
15. Test if the workflows are working.

Hands-on: Run the installation wizard

The following hands-on will demonstrate the installation of Nintex 2010

1. Double-click the installer .msi file to start the installation wizard, which will take you through the steps of asking you to accept the end user license agreement and specify the installation path.

2. Click **Next** to start the Installation Wizard.

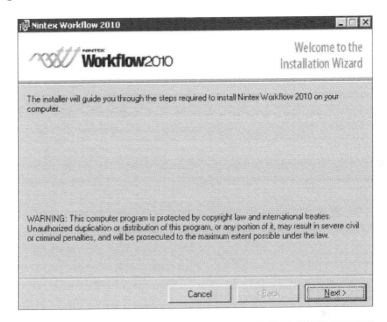

3. Select **I Agree** to agree to the license agreement.

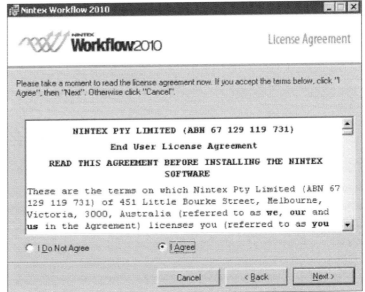

4. Choose the location to install Nintex Workflow and click **Next.**

5. You'll be asked if the solutions can be added to SharePoint directly or that you want to do this on a later moment. Selecting **Yes** causes an IIS Reset so be careful in a production environment.

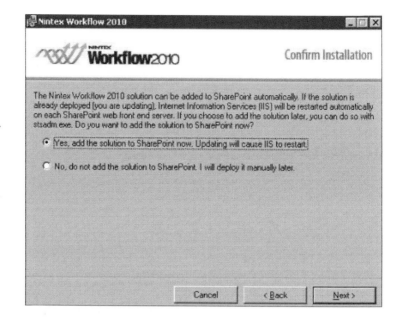

6. Do you want to enable Nintex Live as part of the installation? By enabling this option the installation configures the use of the Nintex Live Framework.

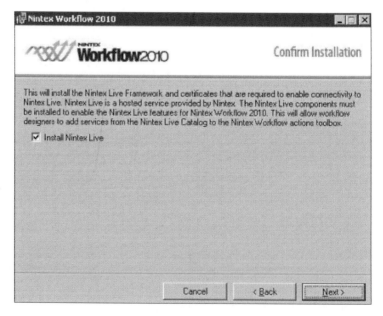

7. Click **Next,**
sit back and wait
for the installation
to complete...

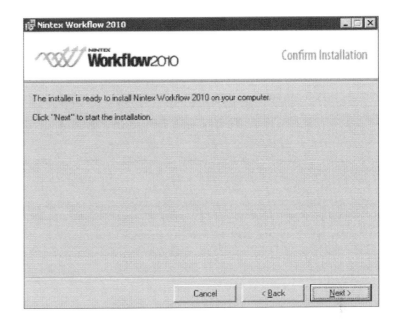

8. If the User Account Control message appears accept this by clicking **Yes.**

9. The installation
is complete,
click **Close.**

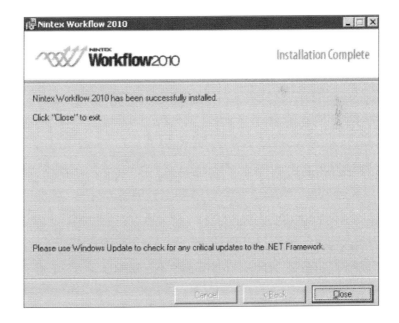

10. Go to Central Administration to activate to the Nintex solution via
System settings, Manage farm solutions.

11. You should see the Nintex solutions there, as shown in the figure below.
    In that figure, we have deployed Nintex Live. Nintex Workflow and Nintex Workflow
    Enterprise are not yet deployed.

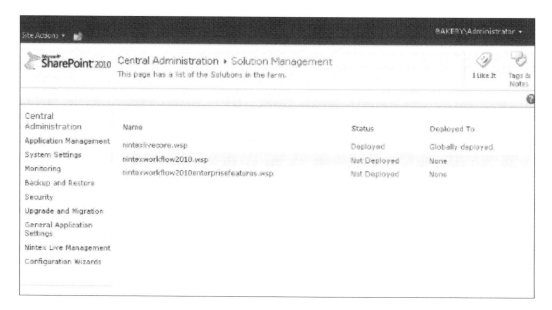

12. For each of the Nintex solutions, click the name of the solution,
    and then click **Deploy Solution**. Select the web application to which you want
    to deploy Nintex Workflow, and choose the time for deployment.

Hands-on: Import the Nintex license
The following hands-on will import the license file
1. Go to Central Administration and select Nintex Workflow Management
2. Click the **Licensing link**, then click **Import**, browse to the license file you
   have received from Nintex
3. Click **Import** to add your license. Your license page should now display
   a nice plaque with your license details.

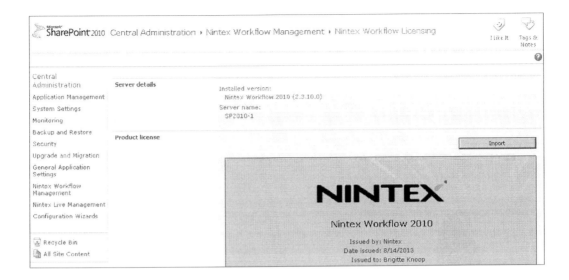

Hands-on: Create database

The following hands-on will create the required Nintex database

1. Go to Central Administration, select **Nintex Workflow Management** and select **Database setup.**
2. Click the **Create** button.
3. You will be asked for the database server, as well as the database name.

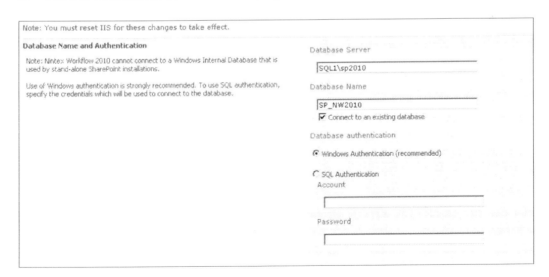

4. Click on **OK** to create the database.

Hands-on: Enable allowed action

The following hands-on will enable the allowed actions

1. Go to Central Administration and select Nintex Workflow Management.
2. Select **Manage Allowed actions.**
3. Click on the Top Left check box to select all actions and click on **OK.**

This list of workflow actions is the default for this farm.

☑ Add a custom action

Category	Name	Description
Integration	Call web service	Send or receive data using a web service
Integration	Create CRM record	Create a new record in a Microsoft Dynamics CRM 4.0 instance
Integration	Delete/Disable CRM record	Delete or disable a record in a Microsoft Dynamics CRM 4.0 instance
Integration	Execute SQL	Execute an SQL command
Integration	Find users by status	Retrieve all users from a group that have a specific OCS/Lync status
Integration	Get user status	Retrieve the OCS/Lync status for a user
Integration	Query BCS	Retrieve data from a Business Connectivity Services data source
Integration	Query CRM	Retrieve records from a Microsoft Dynamics CRM 4.0 instance
Integration	Query Excel Services	Retrieve data from an Excel spreadsheet via Excel Services
Integration	Query LDAP	Retrieve data from an LDAP source
Integration	Query user profile	Retrieve profile properties for a SharePoint user
Integration	Query XML	Retrieve and process XML from a specified source

Hands-on: Activating

The following hands-on will Activate Nintex on the different levels in the farm.

1. Go to Central Administration and select **web application activation**.
2. Select the check box All content web applications and Click on **Activate.**
3. Go to the Site where you want to use Nintex Workflow 2010 and go to the Site Settings page, available from the Site Actions menu.
4. Then, under Site Collection Administration Section select **Site Collection Features.**
5. Enable the Nintex Workflow 2010 feature by clicking on the **Activate** option.

Nintex Workflow - Nintex Live Catalog Allows Nintex Workflow designers to browse the Nintex Live Catalog	Activate
Nintex Workflow 2010 Allow team sites in this site collection to utilize Nintex Workflow features.	Deactivate **Active**
Nintex Workflow 2010 InfoPath Forms Allows Nintex Workflow to use start forms and task forms designed with Microsoft InfoPath 2010.	Activate
Nintex Workflow 2010 Web Parts Allows the Nintex Workflow web parts to be added to sites in this site collection.	Activate
Open Documents in Client Applications by Default Configures links to documents so they open in client applications instead of Web applications, by default.	Activate
PerformancePoint Services Site Collection Features Features enabling the PerformancePoint Services site including content types and site definitions for this site collection.	Activate
Publishing Approval Workflow Routes a page for approval. Approvers can approve or reject the page, reassign the approval task, or request changes to the page. This workflow can be edited in SharePoint Designer.	Activate

6. After activating the site collection Nintex Workflow feature, you can return to the Site Settings page and then select the Manage site features page. You will find a feature named Nintex Workflow 2010.

7. Activate the site feature.

Summary
3 • Setup and Administration

In this chapter we have looked at the installation and configuration of Nintex Workflow on premise and Office 365. Enabling Nintex Workflow on Office 365 takes only a few steps where the on premise steps are more complicated.

We've seen the hardware and software requirements for an onsite installation, and also which permissions you need to have to install the software.
After the installation the license, database and activation are covered. With the action permissions and overall configuration it is time to see the first workflow.

4 • The Workflow Designer

This is where you are going to be a lot, so get yourself acquainted.

Nintex Workflow comes with a workflow editor directly built in so there's no relying on separate programs or hassle with client installations. Nintex Workflow uses SharePoint as the host and your browser as the designer. This means that you do not need to distribute any client programs to authors; as long as they have the proper permissions to the site, they can author and edit workflows.

If you followed the step in the previous chapter you now have a Nintex Workflow environment set up, the administrative tasks are behind us and we can look at all the things that the Nintex designer has to offer.
In this chapter we are going to look at the basics of working with workflows in Nintex Workflow. The Workflow Designer layout will be discussed, adding actions and configuring them, and we save, publish and test your first workflow.
So let's get started!

Your first Nintex Workflow steps

Start your browser and go to your SharePoint environment. If you have created a site with the blank site template, first add a custom list or go into the list of your choice and open the Workflow Settings menu.
You can reach the Workflow Settings menu by clicking in the Top menu on List.

We assume that you have Nintex installed. If not, well you can't create a workflow without installing the software.

In Office 365 click on the Nintex Workflow icon to start the Nintex Workflow app.

When you are using Nintex Workflow for SharePoint click on the arrow at the Workflow Settings menu and choose from the options the "Create a Workflow in Nintex Workflow".

Click Create a Workflow in Nintex Workflow. The Select a Template dialog box should open. Select from the templates the Blank category, select the Blank template and hit the Create button.

The Workflow Designer is loaded, beneath the Nintex Workflow 2010 Designer is displayed.

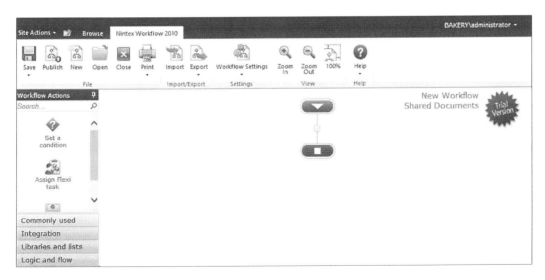

And here is the interface from the Nintex Workflow Designer for Office 365, as you can see the interfaces are almost identical.

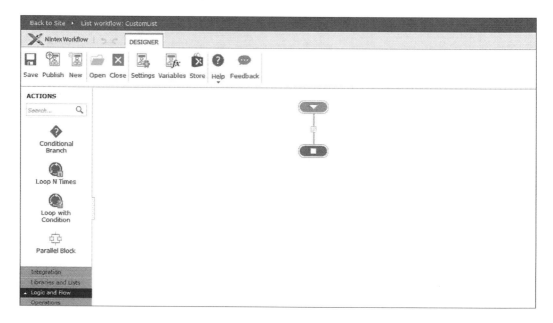

The Workflow Designer page can be divided into three parts:
- The Actions Menu on the left
- The Top Menu on top
- The rest of the space is used for the Canvas.

Actions Menu

First, notice the Workflow Actions menu on the left. This is where you will find all the allowed actions for the current site. You can see more actions by clicking the headlines, such as "Integration", "Libraries and lists", "Logic and flow" and so on.

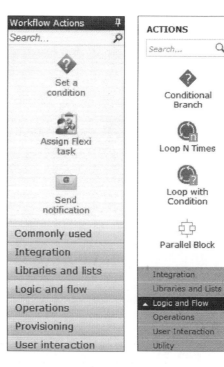

Figure. Action menu's

4 • The Workflow Designer

The pin on the outer site of the Workflow Actions menu is used for setting the Workflow Actions menu to auto hide or always displayed, this option is not available in the Office 365 version.

The dots next to the Workflow Actions menu indicate that you can stretch the Workflow Actions menu. Hover above the dots and if the error signs appear, click your left mouse button and move right. This is especially handy when you have a big screen and want to see more actions.
Finally on the top part of the Workflow Actions menu there is a Search option for searching through the available actions. This is a "type-ahead" search, so even a part of the name already gives a result.

This may also be the first time you notice that not all Nintex Workflow SharePoint actions are available in Nintex Workflow Office 365 version and you are correct. Nintex is still extending the Office 365 version and more actions and options will continue to be added over time.

Top Menu
The top Menu is used for all the general functions of a workflow such as Opening and Closing the workflow, saving it and publishing. The on premise versions have the following extra functions: export a workflow to save it as an external file and import it again. Zoom in on details or zoom out for an overview of the workflow.

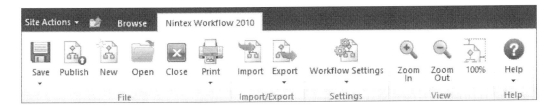

Workflow Settings

The Workflow Settings menu is divided in a Workflow Settings part and a Variables part. In the Workflow Setting dialog screen you can change the title and description. The startup options of the workflow are set here and the lists where history and tasks are written too.

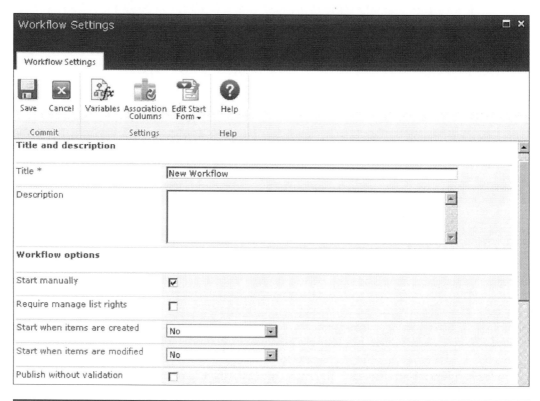

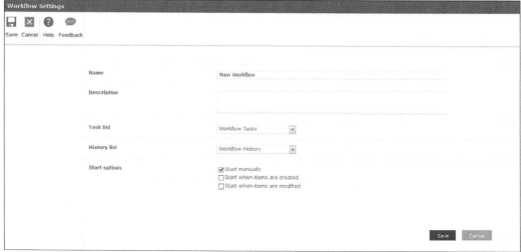

Catalog or Store

If you see a Catalog button then Nintex Live is enabled in your environment. If the button is grey, Nintex Live is not configured or the user doesn't have permissions to use Nintex Live. If the button is orange the user has the right permissions to search for actions from within Nintex Live and then to his workflow. If you want to know more about Nintex Live see the section additional options.

View

In the Top menu you see 2 magnifying glasses and a 100% symbol. These buttons are for the zooming in and out on the workflow or resetting the workflow view back to 100 percent. When creating large workflows these options help you to keep an overview of the entire workflow.

Help

Last in the topmenu list is the Help function which start the help file from Nintex Workflow. And maybe for the first time an IT company has created a very good Help File, with a lot of examples and very extensive. If you ever get stuck in a workflow action you can always have a look in the Help File for support.

Canvas

The canvas is the part where you build your workflows. In the beginning it's easy; the workflow start at the green button and stops add the red button. Always from top to bottom, you can add junctions or parallel tracks in your workflow but the workflow goes from top to bottom.

The gray block is where you add the workflow steps.
On the right side of the canvas screen there is the name of the workflow you are working on and the list or library that this workflows is created in.

Also there is a nice signet telling me that I'm using the Trial Version.
If you buy the full version I'll be sure that Nintex will remove the signet.

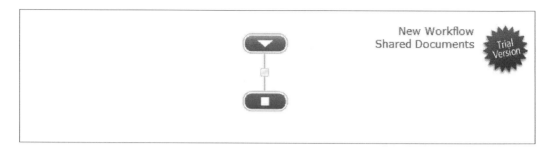

Figure. Canvas layout

Actions

A workflow will only do the things that you tell him to do. You can tell a workflow what to do via workflow steps, these steps are called actions or workflow actions in Nintex Workflow.

You have two options for adding a workflow action:

First, you can drag and drop actions from the Workflow Actions menu on any gray block on the canvas.

Second, you can click a gray action and select the action you want to add from the Insert Action menu that appears, as shown in the figure below.

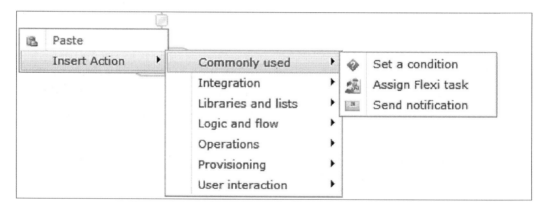

Figure. Insert action menu

If you add an action the canvas will be automatically updated.
Multiple gray blocks will appear, one before the action and one after the action.
Via this way you can add a new action before or after your action. Some actions contain
sub-actions and thus you can add new blocks inside these actions, other actions split
the pad so you can go left or right.

Now let's look at an action, add your first action to the
canvas, the Send notification.
If in theory the workflow now would start, it will begin
at the green button, via the Send notification action and
ends with the red button. When configuring a large and
complex workflow keep in mind that the workflow
always wants to run from top to bottom.

To add more actions to this workflow just drag them from
the actions menu on the left and drop them on the gray
blocks. If you are designing a workflow this is also a
good approach, drag the actions on the canvas that you need to have
and then rearrange them in the correct order by re-dragging them on the canvas.

Almost all actions you place on the canvas need to be configured, you need to tell
the actions exactly what they need to do.
The Send notification action needs to know what he needs to send and to whom.
When you see a yellow exclamation marker in the action you still need to configure that
action. When you hover over the action you see the configuration that need to be done.
An extra warning for preventing workflows to crash: You can save a workflow when not
all actions are configured but you can't publish it.

Figure. Configure warning

To configure an action you can click the title bar and select the configure option from the menu, you can also double-click the action icon. If you select the menu you have a few more options, let's first have a look at these before we configure the action.

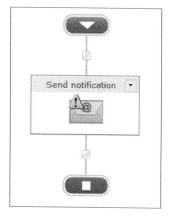

The Action menu allows you to copy the action so you can paste it somewhere else in the current workflow. This is a clever trick if you first configure an action, all settings that are set in that action are also copied into the new action.

With Disable you can exclude the current action from the workflow without deleting it, this can be handy for testing purpose. The Delete option does just that, it deletes the action.

Figure. Action menu

Labels

When you click on the name of the action the view changes to the figure "Edit Labels" and you can add labels on all 4 sides of the action. For example, you can change the title of the action, as well as add text to the left, right, and bottom of the action, as shown in figure "Edit Labels Result".

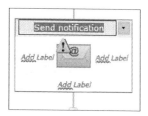

Figure. Edit Labels

Figure. Edit Labels Result

Changing the labels can be useful as you don't have to open an action to view his settings, you can set a properties description in the labels. It's a good practice to have Labels set on all your actions but especially on the actions as "Action set", where you group actions together and "Set a condition" where you can go different ways in the workflow. Setting the correct labels on actions makes it much easier to troubleshoot workflows.

Configure Nintex Workflow local action

Clicking Configure from the Action menu will spawn a Configure Action dialog box. Let's first have a look at the options from a Nintex Workflow 2010 action, we will then look at a Nintex Workflow Office 365 action.

Every action has his own action dialog boxes with options, but once you get to know some of them, you will quickly recognize common dialog box options. The Configure Action dialog box for the **Send notification** action is shown in the Figure Send a notification action config.

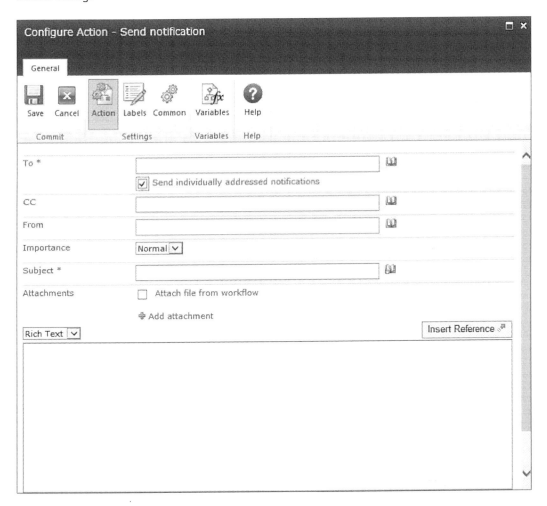

Figure. Send a notification action config

OK, to keep things easy let's move to the menu you see in this action. As indicated the menu options depend on the selected action, the following are in almost all actions.

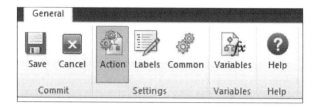

Figure. Action menu

Save and Cancel are the easy ones, these save or cancel the changes you've made to this current action.

The Action button takes you to the specific action configuration, we'll talk about that in a minute.

If you didn't change the name of the labels yet, you can also do it below the button Labels.

The Common button displays the common options of the action. If you don't want the action to appear in reports or in the status reviews, because for example you don't want the user to know what the workflow exactly does, you can set the **Hide from workflow status**. When a user starts the workflow he doesn't see the action, it's executed but not saved in the workflow history. Someone who has to modify workflow permissions can see this action when he edits it.

You can also do the opposite and create an extra log entry after the action completes via the **Message to log on completion** option.

Expected duration

When you design a workflow you also should think about the expected time that workflow should run to complete. You are going to use workflows to automate and hopefully accelerate a business process. If your workflows are running longer than they would do manually, are you then creating the correct workflows?

Setting the expected duration in workflows can help in creating reports about the performance of business processes and the statistics can point to steps where improvements can be made.

The Expected duration can be set in the overall workflow settings for the entire workflow or on all actions individually. The sum of all these single action times together is the time that the workflow is expected to run. Setting the duration per action is of course more accurate but also more complicated to analyze.

Set these times to achievable values, yes an approval can be done in 5 minutes, but a user is not viewing his inbox all day so an approval time of 2 days is more plausible.

Figure. Common options

Variables
The menu item Variables brings you to the place where you can create variables.
You don't know what variables are? Relax we'll get to that soon. For now, the change that Nintex made here are a lot better than in the older version of Nintex workflow 2007 where you first needed to close the action and go to the variables menu before you could create a variable.

Help
If you get stuck in one of these dialog boxes, and it's a good change you will, you can click the Help button on the top right. Contrary to a lot of other software out there the help in Nintex Workflow is very good and gives you a good overview of how to use each configuration dialog box.

Address book

We're now going back to our action tab. The layout of the Send Notification looks a bit like an e-mail application with his To, CC and from. The address book on the right of these fields works also as with an e-mail application, except it has a lot more power.

The address book is divided in three sections:

- Internal Search
- External e-mail address
- Lookup.

The Internal search works as with the other search boxes in SharePoint, type the name of the user and click **Find**. You can also add SharePoint Groups or All Users.

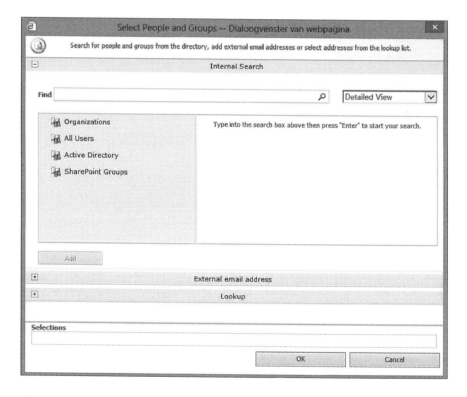

Figure. Select people and groups lookup

The External e-mail address lets you do just that; add an external e-mail address. Take notice that you can't just add an external e-mail address in an approval workflow. The receiver by default doesn't have access to your SharePoint environment so he will receive the approval request but can't approve.

The third selection part is Lookup; with lookups you can use data from the workflow as values in actions or messages. These lookups evaluate when the workflow runs, so their values are dynamic.

The title of the item or the creation date are two values you can use in a lookup, that's not that shocking. But adding the URL of the current item in an e-mail you send to the initiator (both lookups) are very useful.

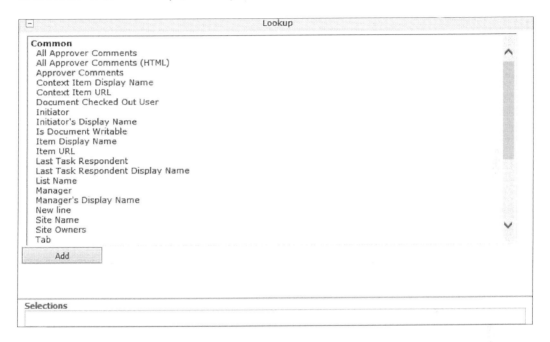

Figure. Lookup value selector

If you create a variable in the workflow or use constants, these are also available in the lookup. Variables and Constants are descibed later in this chapter.

Insert Reference

With Insert References data containing information of the current list item and the current workflow can be used within the workflow actions. The Insert Reference selector is divided into several tabs:

- **Common:** Lookup values containing information about the workflow, the current running item and the current task within the workflow
- **Item Properties:** Metadata columns of the current item and list
- **Workflow Constants:** If there are constants created (other than credentials constants)

they are at this tab. Refer to Workflow Constants later on in this chapter for more information

- **Inline Functions:** Used for additional processing of variables and data. Refer to Inline functions for more info
- **Workflow Variables:** If there are variables created in this workflow they are displayed on this tab. More information about Workflow Variables later in this chapter.

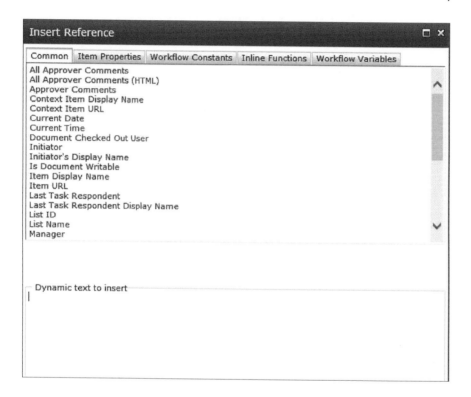

Link Reference

Next to the Insert Reference option there is also the option to create a hyperlink with the workflow data. Select from the top of the menu in the action for the tab Insert and click **Link**.

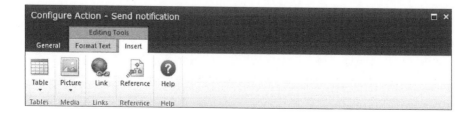

The selector looks much like the Insert Reference we saw a minute ago and is even called so, except that at the bottom there are now two fields instead of one. In the **Address** field the URL link is filled where in the **Hyperlink text to display** field the name of the link is added.

In the screenshot below we added the link from the current item and displayed with the display name.

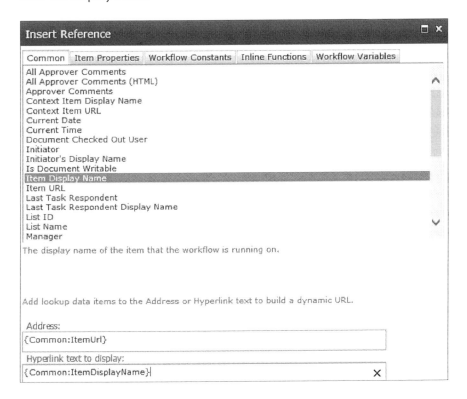

Configure Nintex Workflow Office 365 action

In the Configure Nintex Workflow local action we have looked at the **Send notification,** for Office 365 this action is called **Send an E-mail.**

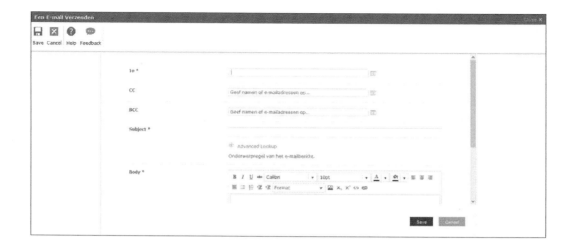

The menus in the Nintex Office 365 actions have lesser options than the on premise versions. The Save and Cancel options are there, also Help in case you're stuck and an optional Feedback, but that's it.

If there are variables that need to be created for an action, you first need to create these outside of the action (For people working a little longer with Nintex, this was indeed the 2007 way).

Address book

The fields TO, CC and BCC are the same as in a normal e-mail only the address book works different. This is not an address book, this is a filter book where you can filter on Workflow Context or list data. In the example below we filtered on the Initiator.

Office 365 limits the send e-mail option to user accounts within the Office 365 environment including registered external users.

All three recipient fields are type ahead or autocomplete aware, entering a part of an account name is enough.

Insert Reference

When the Subject and Body fields are selected, so called free text fields, the Insert Reference section appears at the right sight of the action. Via this section dynamically generated data can be added to the action.

The Insert Reference is divided into three parts:

- **Item Properties**, this is data that is directly linked to the item. Examples are metadata, Creation date or the approval status of the item
- **Workflow Context**, data that is directly linked to the current workflow, the initiator or Workflow name
- **Workflow Variables**, these are the variables that are created in this current workflow.

Variables and Constants

Variables and constants are two different things but they do the same; they can be used to store data. When you are working with workflows you often want to get data, manipulate this data and use it again in another sentence. For example we have a date in a list and want to know how many days this is from today and send that result to someone via e-mail.

This is where you use variables. Variables contain data values that you can use between actions. Variables only contain data as long as the workflow is available. If the workflow ends the variables in that workflow also cease to exist.

The data in the variable is dynamic and can be altered during the processing of a workflow. The data in a variable can only be used in that workflow, if you want to save it you need to write it to a log or field value.

Constants are used for storing values that are set outside the workflow. These constants can be used in several workflows and do not cease to exist when the workflow ends. You cannot change the value of a constant from within a workflow, this must be done from the Nintex Workflow settings menu.

Variables

You can create variables via two ways: one the Workflow Settings in the Top Menu and the second way is via the in almost every action available Variables button. Both will bring you to the Workflow Variables overview.

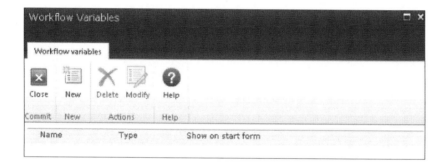

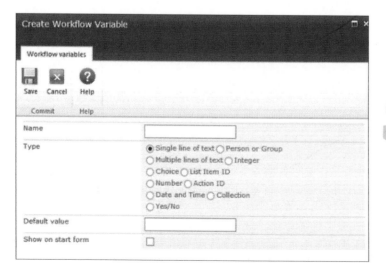

When you create a variable you also need to specify the data type of variable you are using. By defining the data type you are telling the workflow which format the data will have. It's important to use the correct data type as the workflow can't guess what data you are given.

Most data type should be familiar if you are working with SharePoint for a longer time, only the List Item ID, Action ID and Collection may require more clarification.

Every item in a SharePoint list or library has a unique ID in that list, this is the List Item ID. There can be several items with duplicate names in a list but there can't be duplicate ID's. When you are create a new item in a list you can store the List Item ID for future use. When a workflow is running there are several actions that generate an ID. These action ID's can then be used in other actions to follow up. For example an approve action has an Action ID set, then a reminder action can be triggered on this Action ID.

A collection variable is a variable that contains a collection of single workflow variables, these single variables can be from any type of variable type. A collection can only have one type of variables, there is no option to mix a text value with an number value.

If you have developed you may see constants as an area.

Constants

This option is not available in the Office 365 version of Nintex Workflow.

Constants can be used for storing strings, numbers, date, credentials and secure strings. You can for example save the URL of an ERP system that you often use in a workflow. As Nintex Workflow doesn't work with Secure Store Applications, constants can be used to achieve this function.

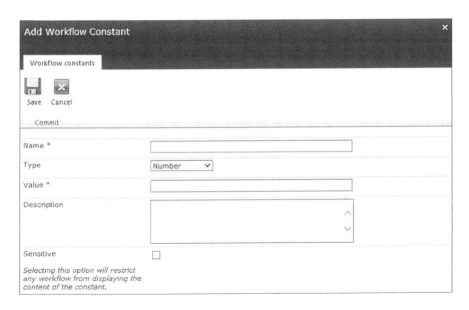

When a constant is saved you can add a reference to that constant in a workflow and users can connect with that username and password.

Go to edit a workflow task, you can now look up the constant and use it for configuring the action, as shown in the picture below

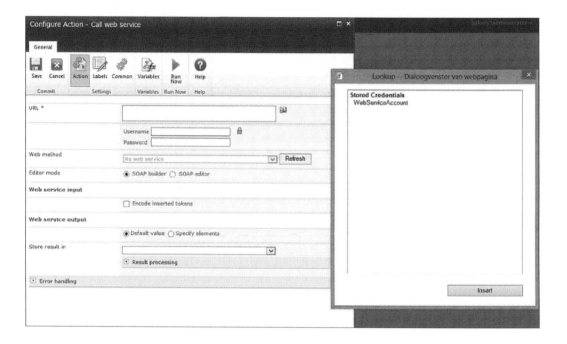

Saving and publishing your workflow

We have created a workflow with just one action. It's a small start, but it's a start. Now we are going to save the workflow and publish it to make it available for the users to use.

In the Top menu in the toolbar of your Workflow Designer there is the option called Publish. Clicking this item the workflow will check if all actions are correctly configured and then make the workflow available for users.

If the workflow isn't available for publishing because you're not yet finished, you can save the workflow. When only saving a workflow, it can't be executed; the workflow also doesn't check if all actions are configured.

If the workflow is saved or published for the first time, Nintex Workflow will ask for the Title of the workflow. As a best practice always add a correct description of what the workflow does. If you then after six months need to maintenance it, you can still find out what the workflow does.

Hands-on: Create your first workflow

1. Browse to a library or list where you want to create a workflow.
2. Select from the Top Menu the option **Library**.
3. From the workflow options pull down,
   select the **Create a Workflow in Nintex Workflow** option.

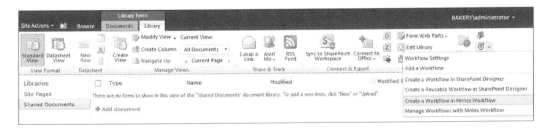

4. From the template selection select **Blank** and click on **Create**.
5. From the "Commonly used" category of the Workflow Actions menu,
   drag the **Send Notification** action to the first grey block.

6. Double-click on the action to configure it.

7. Enter your username in the To field.

8. Add some text in the Subject field and the Body field.

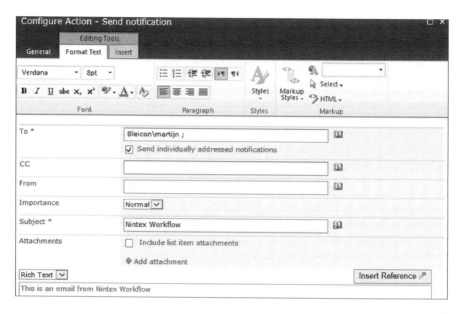

9. Click on the General tab, followed by the **Save** option.

10. Click in the Top Menu on **Publish**.

11. Give the workflow the name **Send e-mail**.

12. It's a good practice to use descriptions so also add a description and submit the workflow.

Summary
4 • The Workflow Designer

In this chapter we've looked at the layout of the Workflow Designer with his top menu, action menu and canvas. The first action was added to the workflow and we configured this. Finally we saved the workflow and published it.

5 • Simple workflows

We've seen the basics, now let's continue small.

In the previous chapter we have looked at the real basics of working with Nintex Workflow. Now we are going further and are going to use other Nintex Workflow actions. We start with the most requested workflow and used in almost any business; the approval workflow.

Approval

The approval workflow is a workflow where a user requests an approval to another user. This can be for example a request for a day-off, a purchase, or the approval of a report. SharePoint has by default a few out of the box workflows where the approval workflow is one of them. So why would someone use an external application for the approval when there is an off the shelf version? Well the approval options in SharePoint are limited, if you want to send a user a friendly reminder about the task that is waiting his approval, you can't. The option to escalate an approval workflow is not available in SharePoint as also the option to gather the response from other people before setting the request on behalf of the group.

For all the above options we can use Nintex workflow and in the following chapter we show you how.

Open a new Nintex workflow by following these steps: go to a library and select from the top menu the tab **Library**. Then all the way to the right select the workflow icon menu and select **Create a Workflow in Nintex Workflow**. Select the **Blank template** and click **Create**.

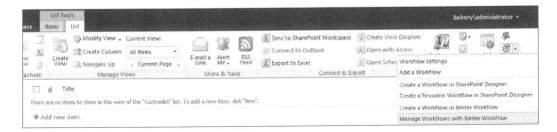

Drag from the actions menu the action **Assign Flexi task**.

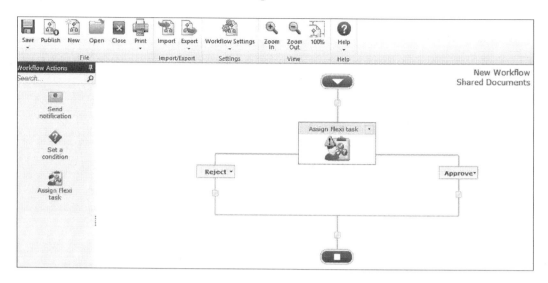

You see that the layout automatically adjusted to the action,
the **Assign Flexi task action** has two possible outcomes, a **Reject**
or **Approve** and the workflow paths are adjusted to these option.

If you would add another
Assign Flexi task action
in the Approve or Reject path
this will again split up
and so on and so on.
Open the action by
double-clicking on the action.
The available options in this
action are different than
the ones we have seen in
Send a Notification.

The **Assignees** field works
the same way as the **To** field
in Send Notification, the **Task
description** field can be seen
as the body field of the

Send Notification action. With the **Outcomes** field you can add extra outcomes which users can choose from.

The **Behavior** field lets you choose what the workflow does when your approvers approve or reject the workflow. See below the options there are.

Behaviour		
	⦿ First response applies	◯ Majority decides
	◯ Majority must choose a specific outcome	◯ All must agree
	◯ All must agree on a specific outcome	

After adding Assignees you can save the action and publish the workflow.

When you now start the workflow Nintex Workflow will create a task for every assignee and send an e-mail to these users that there is a task assigned to him/her.

But what if users don't respond to the tasks that where assigned to them, because they are sick or on a much-needed holiday? Are we going to wait till they get back or can we let someone else do the task for them?

Escalation

In Nintex it's easy to create an escalation and it is even part of a flexi task action.

An escalating workflow action will basically perform some action if another action has not happened for a given period of time.

For example, you may assign a workflow task to an employee that always needs to be completed in 5 days, and then that employee gets sick. Your planning would fail if we didn't escalate this.

In this case, an escalating workflow is able to take control of a task after a given period of inactivity and delegate the task to either another employee, a group of employees, or a manager.

You can also choose to complete the task. You can set up this to happen after any time period, even excluding weekends and holidays, as shown in the figure on the next page.

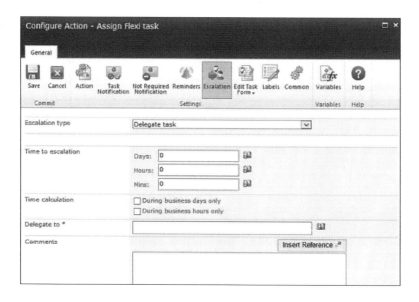

Delegating task

Open the flexi-task action and go to the Escalation tab, select **Delegate task**.

The required field **Delegate to** should be self-explanatory and contains the user to which the task should be delegated. The best method here is to make this as dynamic as possible, so try if you can first retrieve the manager of the user in a variable and then set this variable in the **Delegate to** box.

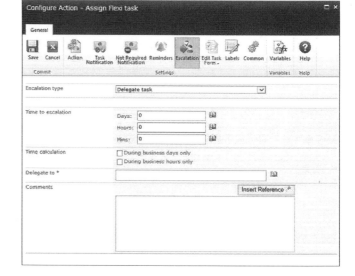

The **Time to escalation** period you define here is the wait time before the task is delegated. It's best to set this time to a reasonable period, using a short time period maybe fastens the task process but isn't representative for your organizational processes.

Complete task

There are processes that need to be completed within a specific time, for example an objection period. If the approvers don't react within that time, the workflow action will complete and the workflow will continue. You can set the Outcome field to a specific value and for example reuse this later in the workflow to count the amount of completed tasks.

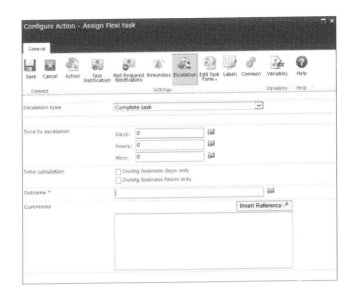

Reminders

So we now know what we can do to escalate a task in Nintex Workflow. But maybe the user is just very busy and he forgot he had a task waiting his approval, are we going to escalate that? Why not just send him first a reminder that there is a workflow task awaiting his approval?

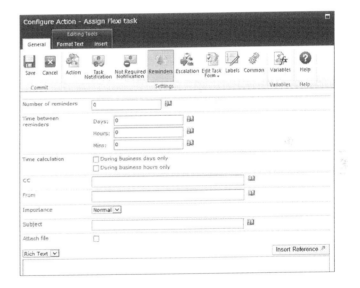

Next to the Escalation tab is the Reminders tab in the flexi-task action. Here you can set the amount of reminders that a user receives in which time period. Set this to a reasonable time in which you want a person to remind him. Setting a reminder every 10 minutes seems in the beginning fun but what if your CEO is the one that needs to approve and his mailbox explodes with your reminders?
Setting the reminder after a week and then every 3 days is a more elegant way to remind someone.

Reminders and escalations timing

You now have two settings in the flexi-task action that work with time, so this is a good time to talk about timing in workflows. Workflows that require a time period are run by a timer job in SharePoint. This timer job is default set to run every 5 minutes if the hardware resources at that moment allow. If your environment is overcommitted and peaking at 100% the timer job may be delayed for a few minutes.
If you set a workflow therefore to wait for 1 minute don't look surprised if it takes
5 minutes, the maximum that we have seen is a "one minute" that took 12 minutes.

Another point to notice is that the time periods of reminders and escalation are counted as one. So setting a reminder after 2 days and an escalation after 3 days doesn't make the workflow wait for 5 days, the workflow sends a reminder after 2 days and the next day sends an escalation.

Start data variables

In some workflows you want to use values that you can't calculate or that you don't have. With start data variable you can ask these at the workflow initiator. For example you want to know with type of project document you created so the project manager of that project can approve. If you don't store this data in workflow you can simply ask the user who needs to approve the workflow.
Go to variables and set the option Show on start form, if needed you can also make it **Required**.

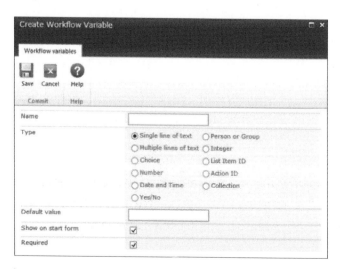

Because the user needs to insert information before the workflow starts, you can only ask start data variables on workflows that are started manually. For workflow that are started automatically you need to use another method like the action "Request data".

Set workflow options

This is a nice bridge to tell something about the workflow start options that are available in Nintex Workflow. Under the Workflow settings menu item there is a section called **Workflow options** and it's here where you can set the three default start-up options in Nintex:

- **Start manually**; every workflow needs to be started manually, meaning by hand or from within another workflow
- **Start when items are created**; when a new item is added to the current library or list this workflow is started
- **Start when items are modified;** If an item is modified this current workflow will be started. If the list contains version history the restore to a previous version also is seen as an update resulting in the start of the workflow.

The option to start a scheduled workflow can't be configured here, more information about that will come in the chapter **Creating advanced workflow**.

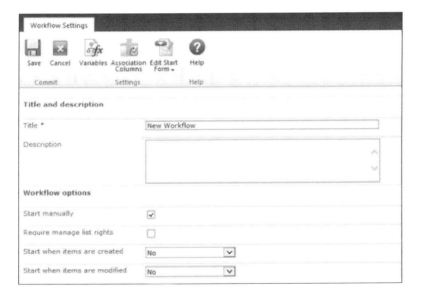

Set field values

In the beginning of this chapter we started with an approval action; if we would start a workflow, this action will ask approval to a specific user or group. When the action is completed the workflow will continue and because this is the only action in the workflow the workflow will end.

The only problem is that the user could approve but the item isn't approved. Remember when we said that you have to tell the workflow everything that he needs to do? We now have to tell the workflow to update the current item approval field with the outcome of the approval request.

Set approval status

Add the **Set approval status** action from the **Libraries and lists** section to both paths (Reject and Approve) of the **Assign Flexi task** action.

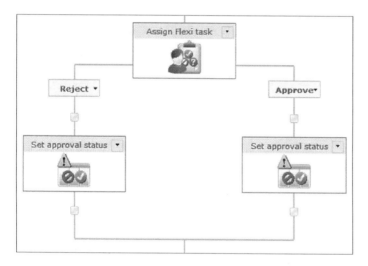

You can set the outcome of the approval status in this action, in the **Reject** path you would choose to set the **Set the status to** field to Rejected, where in the **Approve** path this will be set to Approved.

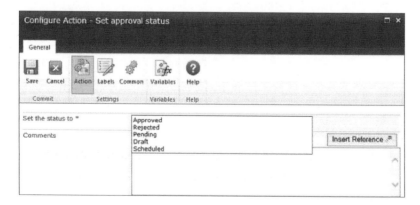

5 • Simple workflows

If the document library where this workflow is running is set **to require content approval for submitted items**, the items are now visible for all users when the outcome of the workflow is approved.

Set field value / Update item

The **Set field value** is used for updating a field on the current item. The value can be "a hard coded" entry or a dynamically value from a workflow variable or constants, list lookup, workflow context or the user profile service.

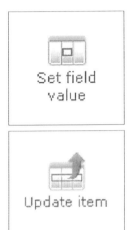

The **update item** makes it possible to update several fields in an item in a list on the current site. The first part of the workflow is a query part where a select query is created to retrieve the item to update, the second part is for the fields that need to be updated.

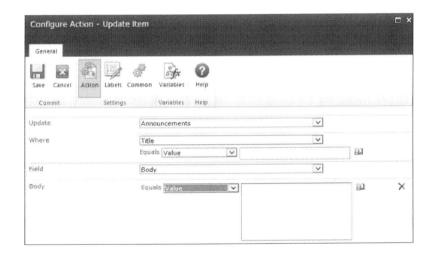

Working with libraries and lists

When a user approves a task you can let the workflow change a field or update an item. But as Nintex Workflow is fully integrated in SharePoint there are lot more options you can do with items, libraries and lists.

Here are some actions that let you interact with lists and libraries.

Create item

The **Create item** action is used for creating an item a list or library in the current site. All available lists and libraries are selectable from the **Create item** in field. When the correct list is selected the corresponding **Content types** of that list are loaded.

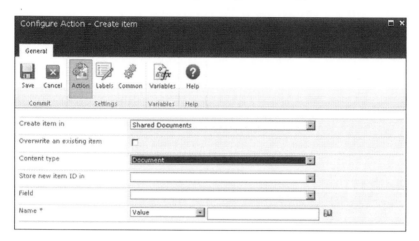

Any field from the current content type can be selected to be filled with data, as you can see on the image below. Don't forget that the required fields are filled. Also the data type of the variables that are used must match the field type of the field that is to be set.

When you don't want to create an item in this site use the Create item in another site action.

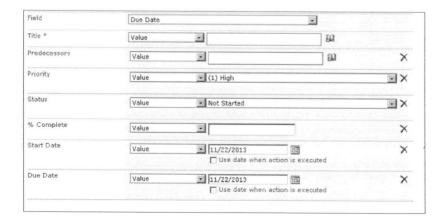

The **Create item** action could be used to create a list item to save the result of an approval workflow for future references.

Copy item

If you want to create a copy of an item you should use the **Copy item** action. The default action is you copy the current item. But via selections you can copy any item in the current site to another list in the current site. There's also the option to overwrite the item if it already exists.

If the item needs to be created in another site you have to use a web service, more info about this in section: **Working with External sources**.

Query list

For retrieving data from another list use the **Query list** action.
The query for retrieving data can be built via 2 methods:
The Query builder option where the filters via fields and variables can be combined or the CAML editor can be used with the CAML query language.

> **For more info about using the CAML query:**
> **http://msdn.microsoft.com/en-us/library/office/ms467521.aspx**

The results that are returned from the query can be more than a single item. Therefore the action also contains a sort option where you can select to sort the results on fields ascending or descending.

In the Field selection field you select the fields that you want to retrieve from the query and then the variable where you want the result to store in. This action contains a **Run Now** option to be used to test the query and results.

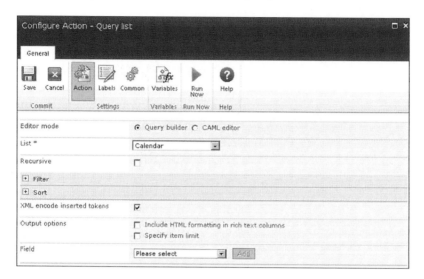

An example that is often used for using the query list action; in the current list is a choice field that resembles a choice field in another list. By selecting a choice from the current list you filter on the items in the other list.

Let's say we have a list that is used for requesting information in a company via an attached InfoPath form. A field in that form represents the department from whom you want information. When the InfoPath form is filled in and saved, the workflow will match this department field with the other list and retrieve the e-mail address that matches the department field. Via this structure you can create flexible solutions as there is no data hardcoded in the workflow. If the e-mail address of the department changes only the corresponding list needs to be updated.

Set item permissions

If an article or document is approved then you most likely want that not everybody can alter the item. This can be prevented by changing the item permissions of that item.

Changing the permissions of items on item level is in most cases not recommended as this creates a to fine grained permissions and results in an uncontrollable rights overview.

Setting permissions via a workflow is an exception because the steps are set in a repeatable way resulting always in the same permissions per phase.

The first part of the action **Set permission** on is the same as with the previous actions. Do you want the permissions to change on this item or on the another item that you select via a query?

The second part is used to specify to inherit the permission or remove them. This action could therefore also be used to restore the permissions that were removed in another stage of the workflow. Remove existing permission does exactly that and removes all permissions. If this is used incorrectly you can't access the item anymore and you need to contact an administrator to reset the permissions. Administrators always keep their permissions.

Setting permissions on a list or library requires the use of the permissions web service.

You can set the permissions on user and group based where of course groups are preferred; you can here also use variables that contain users or groups.

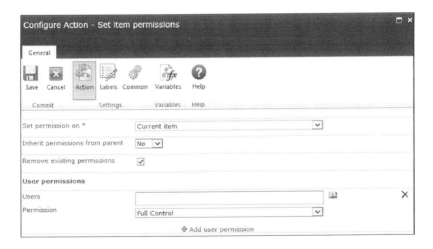

Create list
If an item creating isn't enough, you can also create a whole list via one single action, here we use the **Create list** action.

The **Title** and **Description** fields are self-explanatory, the List template may require some more explanation. Every standard SharePoint list is based on a template. With these templates you can easily create a list from a specific type with all the required corresponding columns and views. Default lists are for example a Calendar list, a document library and a task list.

There is the option to create the list at the current **URL** or on a different location. As this may require other permissions, an additional **Username** and **Password** can be provided in the **Override credentials** section.

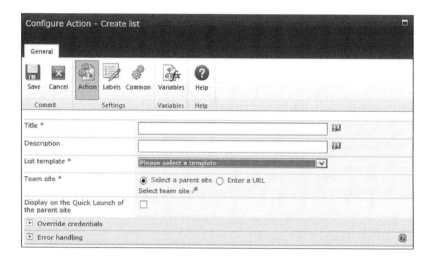

For information about using the Error handling option see chapter Working with external sources.

Review workflow

Nintex has a function that is great for viewing the path your workflow has followed. That way you can for example see who approved the workflow or how long it has taken to complete. The only problem about the function is that it isn't easy to find. The option is hidden in the menu option View Workflow History on the item context menu, as shown on the next page.

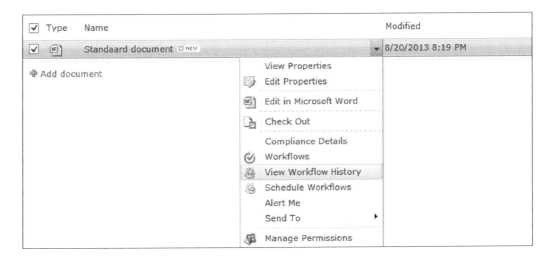

You are redirect to a page where you can view all workflows that have run on that list item. In the image below you can see that we have run several workflows on a single item and some of them completed; but also some got cancelled or ran into an error. Clicking on the link will bring you that workflow history.

We have clicked on a workflow as shown below; this workflow only contains a single action. Nintex workflow uses colors to display which steps and route the workflow has followed.

The green colored actions represent the actions that are completed, the gray actions represent the action that are not executed.

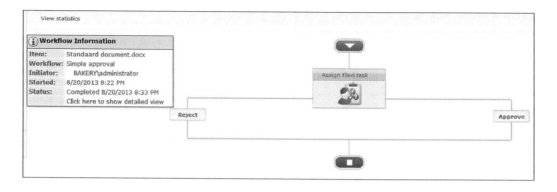

Do you want to know an even better function of workflow reviewing? You can view the workflow history also on workflows that are running at this moment.
The workflow below is running and if this book was printed in color you could see the green and gray colored actions, the yellow actions represents actions that are being processed at this moment.

If a workflow is running longer than expected you can have a look in the workflow history and see what causes the workflow to keep running; in the image below the workflow is waiting for an approval.

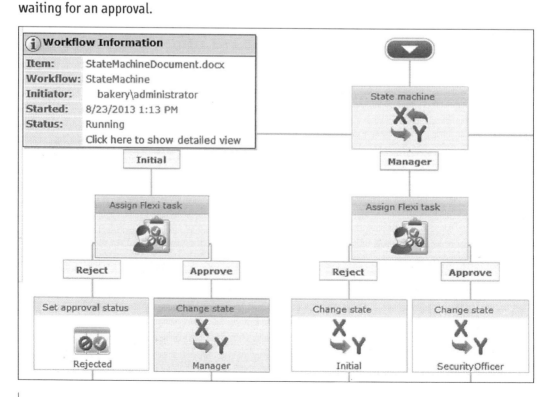

Statistics

Measuring is knowing (and knowing often doesn't change a thing). We know how a workflow has run on a single item. But what if you want to know how long a workflow ran on all items, or the average approval time from your users?

We can use the workflow statistics to view the statistics of workflows and if it is required, change the expected durations or the escalation options in the workflow. You can reach the workflow statistics via a detour that goes via the Site Settings page, under the Nintex Workflow section select **Workflows gallery**. All workflows created at this site are displayed and in the top section is the **View statistics** option.

The image below displays the statistics of a workflow and can be used to view the overall duration of the workflow and how often each step has run.

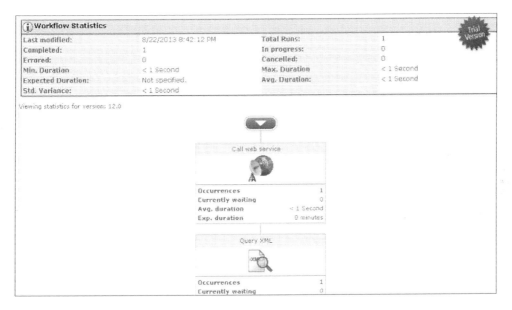

On the page there is also action-specific information, for example, the "Assign Flexi task" action shows how many times a user responded to the request and what the outcome was of that response.

Hands-on: Create an approval workflow

The following hands-on will create a workflow

1.   Browse to a library or list where you want to create a workflow.
2.   Select from the Top Menu the tab **Library**.
3.   From the workflow options pull down select
      Create a Workflow in Nintex Workflow.

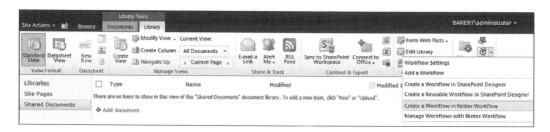

4.   From the template selection select **Blank** and click on **Create**.
5.   From the **Commonly used** category of the Workflow Actions menu,
      drag the **Assign Flexi task** action to the first gray block.

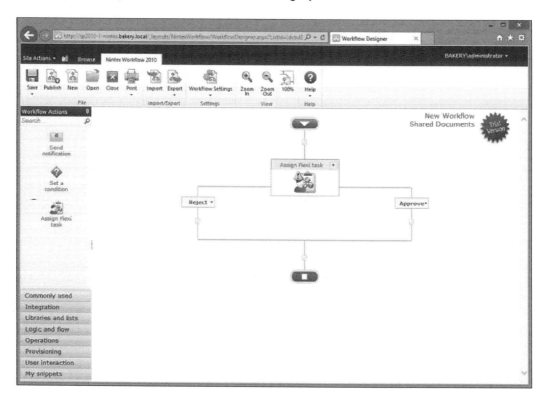

6. Next, click the arrow on title bar of the action, and select **Configure from the menu**.
7. In the **Approvers** field, click the address book button to search for the username. Search for the current logged on user as approver.
8. Scroll down and hit **Save** to complete configuring the action.
9. In the top menu bar select **Publish**.
10. Give the workflow the name **Simple Workflow** and click **Submit**.
11. When the message appears that the workflow is saved click **OK**.
12. Return to the Library and upload a document.
13. Hover above the document and select from the pull-down the option **Workflows**.

14. Click under **Start a New Workflow** the **Simple approval** workflow.
15. Click the **Start** button

Hands-on: Approve an workflow

The following hands-will approve the workflow you've created in the previous step.

1. Browse to the library where you started the workflow.
2. Click the **In Progress** link.

Type	Name		Modified	Modified By	Simple approval
🖹	Standaard document 🗅 NEW		8/20/2013 8:19 PM	BAKERY\administrator	In Progress

3. Hover above the Workflow task and select from the pull-down for the option **Edit Item**.

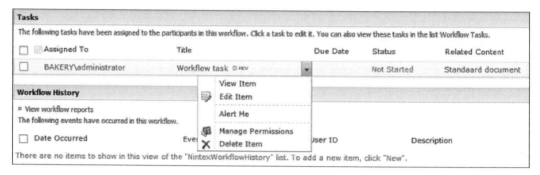

4. Select **Approve** and Click on **OK**.

Hands-on: Create a workflow with escalation

The following hands-will update the workflow with an escalation

1. Browse to the library where you created the workflow.
2. Choose from the workflows menu for the option **Manage Workflows with Nintex Workflow**.

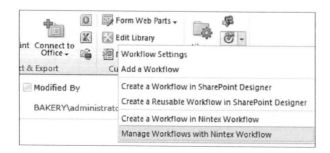

3. Select the workflow **Simple approval.**
4. Double-click on the **Assign Flexi task** action and click on **Escalation.**
5. Select from the escalation type select **Complete task.**

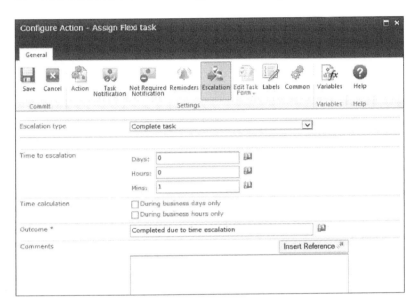

6. Set the time to escalation to 1 minute by entering 1 in the field **Mins.**
7. Set the following text in **outcome: completed due to time escalation.**
8. Click on **Save.** And **Publish** the workflow.
9. Return to the library.
10. Hover above the document and select from the pull-down
    the option **Workflows.**
11. Click under Start a New Workflow the **Simple approval workflow.**
12. Click the **Start** button.
13. Wait 5 minutes and refresh the browser.
14. The workflow is set to completed.

Hands-on: Create a workflow with startup options

The following hands-will adjust the workflow with an startup option

1. Return to the previously created workflow named **Simple workflow.**
2. From the menu bar click **Workflow Settings** and **Variables.**

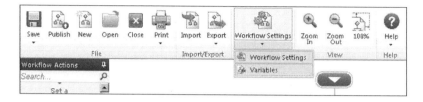

3. Click **New**.

4. In the **Name** field fill in **StartupApprover**.
5. Default user is the **administrator** or your username.
6. Check the boxes **Show on start form** and **Required**.
7. Click on **Save**.
8. Remove in the **Assignees** field the users and click on the **address book**.
9. Go to the section lookup and then all down under **Workflow Variables** select **StartupApprover**, click on **Add** and then **OK**.

5 • Simple workflows

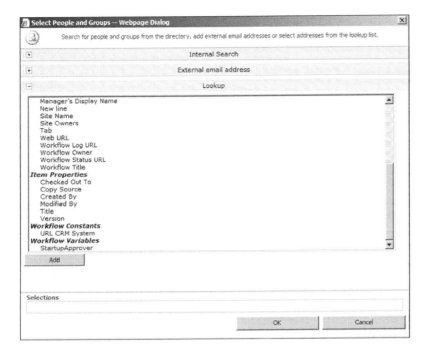

10. Click on **Save** to close the action.

11. Click in the menu bar for **Publish** to save the workflow, click on **Save**.

12. When the message appears the workflow is saved click **OK**.

13. Return to the library and start the workflow via item menu and workflows.

14. Select **Start a new workflow**.

15. Select a new user or accept the default user and click on **Start**.

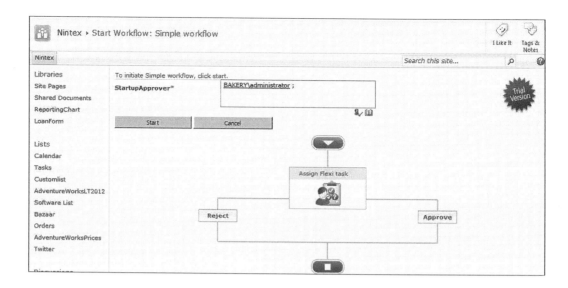

Hands-on: Create a workflow with more steps

The following hands-will create a workflow with several steps.

1.   Return to your library and go to the library settings.

2.   Select the option **Versioning Settings**.

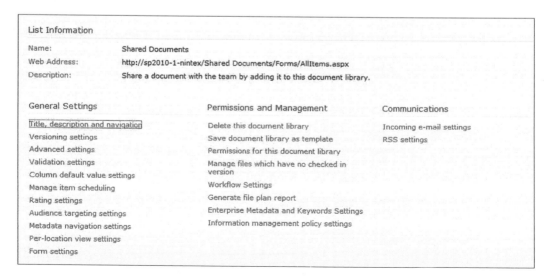

3. Set the option Require content approval for submitted items? To **Yes**.
4. For Document Version History Set the option **Create major and minor (draft) versions**.
5. Click on **OK**.
6. Return to the library.
7. Choose from the workflows menu for the option **Manage Workflows with Nintex Workflow**.
8. Select the **Simple Workflow**.
9. Double-click the **Assign Flexi task**.
10. Go to the Escalation tab and set the Escalation type to **None**.

11. **Save** the action.
12. From the list of actions click on **Libraries and lists**.
13. Select **Set approval status** and drag it under the section **approve**.

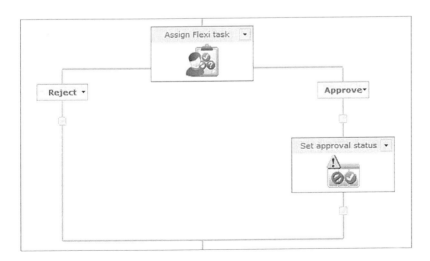

14. From the action menu click on **Copy**.

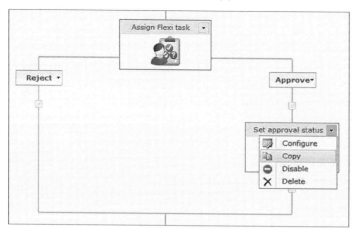

15. On the left side of the workflow beneath Reject click on **the gray square** and choose **Paste**.

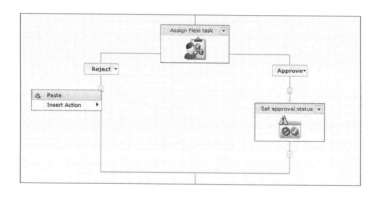

16. Your page will now look like this.

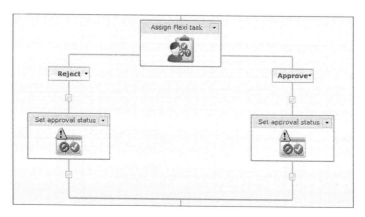

17. Now configure the actions, double-click on the **Set Approval status** action.
18. Set the value Set the status to on the right side to **Approved** and the left side to **Rejected** and click on **Save**.

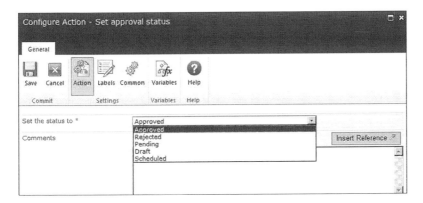

19. The text beneath the approval actions are now set to Rejected and Approved.
20. Click on **Publish**.
21. Click on **Submit** and **OK**.
22. Start the workflow and on the approval task choose **Reject**.
23. The Approval Status is set to **Rejected**.

	Type	Name	Modified	Modified By	Simple approval	Approval Status
		Rotterdam Marathon training	12/13/2013 10:38 AM	bakery\administrator		Pending
		StateMachineDocument	5/23/2014 9:41 AM	bakery\administrator		Rejected

Hands-on: Create a leave request workflow

In this hands-on we will create a leave request workflow to help simplify the approval process for employees. The workflow will Send a notification to the requestor, send a request for approval to his or her manager. If the manager declines the user is informed, on approval the user also receives a message.

Create the Leave List

Create a new list named **Leave**. Ensure that following columns are available in the SharePoint list:

- **Leave Type**; choice field with the following options
  - o   Annual leave
  - o   Sick leave
  - o   Maternity leave
- **Start Date**; date and time field
- **End Date**; date and time field
- **Description**; multiple lines of text.

Create the Leave Request Workflow
1. Create a new workflow.
2. Select **Blank template** and click **Create**.
3. Select and drag from the common section on the left action menu the **Send Notification** workflow action onto the design canvas.
4. Double-click the **Send Notification** action to open the configuration dialog.
5. In the **To** field, click the Lookup icon.
6. Select the Lookup section and click **Initiator**.
7. Click **Add** and **OK**.
8. In the Subject field, type **Your leave request**.
   a. Select the **Insert Reference icon**
   b. In the Item Properties tab, click **Leave Type**
   c. Type the following text in the Subject field **is received**
   d. The text in the Subject is now:
      Your leave request *Leave Type* is received.
9. In the e-mail body text box, type the following message "Your leave request has been received and *Manager's Display Name* is going to review your request."

Note: The Manager's Display Name is an Reference field.

10. Type **Leave information** into the textbox and then **Type** on the next line
11. Click on the **Insert Reference icon**.
12. Select the **Item Properties** tab.
13. Select **Leave Type** and then **OK**.
14. Press the return button to start on a new line.
15. Repeat the steps to insert the **Start Date**, the **End Date** and **Description**.
16. Click on the **General tab** and then **Save**.

Configure a request approval action for the Manager

1. Drag a **Request Approval** action below the **Send notification** action.
2. Double-click on the **request approval** action to configure the action.
3. In the **Approvers** field, click the Lookup icon.
4. Select the Lookup section and click **Manager**.

Note: the function Manager requires that the manager information is configured in the Active Directory account of the initiator.

5. Click **Add** and then **OK**.
6. In the **Ribbon**, click **Task Notification**.
7. In the Edit settings for field, select **Manager**.
8. In the Subject field, type the text **Approval required**.
9. Click on the General tab and then **Save**.

Send an e-mail to notify the initiator when request is denied

Configure a send notification to inform the initiator that his leave request is rejected.

1. Drag a **Send Notification** action on the left-hand side
   of the request approval workflow action.
2. Double-click the action to configuration it.
3. In the **To** field, click the **Lookup** icon to enter the **Initiator**.
4. In the Subject field, select the **Insert Reference icon**.
   a. In the Item Properties tab click on **Leave Type** and then **Add**.
   b. Type has **been rejected** after the Leave Type value.
   c. The text in the Subject is now: *Leave Type* has been rejected.
5. In the e-mail body text box, add some text.

Send an e-mail to notify the initiator when request is approved

Copy the Send Notification from the previous step to use in the approve path

1. Click on the menu from the previous configured action and select from the menu **copy**.
2. Click on the grey block beneath the right sight of the approval
   and select **Paste** from the menu.
3. Double-click on the action to open the configuration dialog.
4. In the Subject field, replace the text rejected by the word approved.
   a. The text in the Subject is now: *Leave Type* has been approved.
5. In the e-mail body text box, add some text.

Save and Publish the workflow

6. In the Top Menu, click **Publish**.
7. In the Title field, type "Leave Request Process".
8. In the Description field, type "Use this workflow to process leave requests".

Advanced Hands-on: Extra leave request options

Continue on the previous created workflow and try to add the following options into the workflow.

- If the leave request is approved by the manager there is an item created in a SharePoint calendar so colleagues can see that the user is away (**Create item action**).
- Try if you can change the permissions so the initiator can't change the request after the manager has approved.
- If the leave request type is sickness no item is created in the calendar due to privacy of the employees (use the **Set a condition** or **Run if** action).

Summary

5 • Simple workflows

In this chapter we started with our first real workflow: the approval workflow. This is the workflow that is used the most and as you can see very easy to create. We extended this workflow with the available escalation options and looked at the reminders. We used start data variables in the workflow to request information from the user. After the approval section we used that outcome to set field values with the approval status and other metadata.

In the upcoming chapters there are a lot of actions that still can be used for an approval workflow, the advanced hands-on task that prevents the creation of an item when the leave type is sickness is just one example. By practicing with these basic workflow types you set a good basis for featuring more complex workflows.

6 • Creating advanced workflows

In the last section we created a few approval workflows.
We hope that this wasn't that complicated and that we
can move-on and have a look at the more advanced workflows.
In this section we are going to look at many actions used for advanced workflows,
the scheduling of workflows, advanced actions and saving workflows as snippets
or templates.

Structural actions

Creating more advanced workflows requires also more advanced workflow actions.
The following actions are used to bring logic, structure and flow into your workflows
and are therefore important to know.

Conditions

The **Set a condition** is an action that's often used, and it's therefore that Nintex placed this
action also in the commonly used section. Conditions are used to have choices in your
workflow: "if this field is set to this value then follow this path otherwise follow this path".

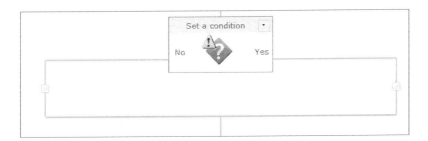

An example, if the total amount of a purchase is above the 10.000 euro the CEO needs
to approve the purchase, otherwise the manager may approve the acquisition.
In this example you would at a Set a condition action and set in both outcomes
an approval action, one for the manager and one for the CEO.

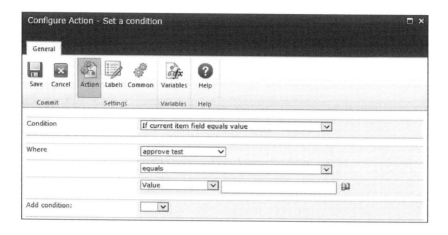

Set a condition works with look-ups; this can be a look-up to the current item, an item in another list on the same site, workflow variables or constants or a user profile. You can't get data from outside the current site with this action, therefore you need to use web services. We get to web services later on in this book.

If you change the condition the rest of the fields will dynamically change with the type of data you want to retrieve.

Do not try to build a workflow where every option from a choose field value is captured into a nested **Set a condition** configuration as this creates very messy workflows. The best is to use a state machine workflow for this type of workflow.

Run if

The **Run if** action looks at first almost the same as the **Set a condition** action. Where the condition action the workflow splits into two different outcomes, the **Run if** action sets the corresponding block that need to be executed if the condition is true, otherwise that block is ignored.

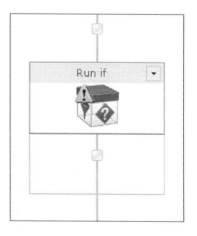

Run if is mostly used for small side steps in a workflow. For example if a user checked a box **Send e-mail** you can set a **Run if** action that checks if that box is ticked and then sends an e-mail.

For each

With the **For each** action you can loop through to each value in a collection variable. You can add other actions as child actions of the **For each** action, and these actions will be executed for each value in the collection. The current value of the collection is accessible to each of the child actions via a workflow variable.

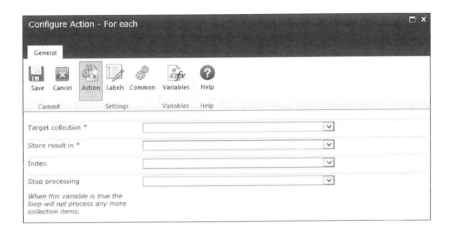

The Index field can be used to count the current position in the collection, the first value is 0.

Stop processing can be filled with a Yes/No variable that can break the **For each** loop.

An example where you could use the **For each** action for could be to let your SharePoint users know that their site is going into maintenance. You would query the site to get all users in a variable collection and then for each user in that collection send an e-mail to that user.

Loop

The Loop action is an action that runs a set of child actions while a condition is true; if the condition is false the loop stops and the workflow continues.

You can see in the image that the values that you can set are the same as with the Set a condition action. That's because this action also uses a check on the values that are set.

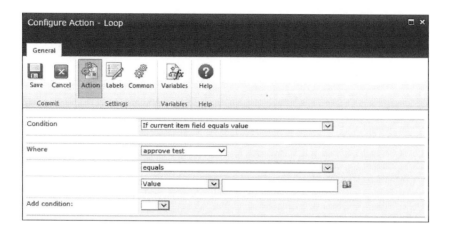

Filter

An action that also works the same as the **Set a condition** action is the **Filter** action. With the **Filter** action the workflow will end if the configured condition is not met.

Action Set

The **Action Set** action is a container where you can bundle your actions in and that can be collapsed and expanded. If you label this **Action Set** with a good description, you can order your workflow. You can also directly save the **Action Set** as a snippet.

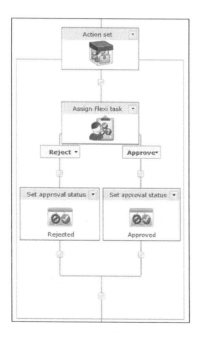

Operational actions

As a developer once told me: "Programming is nothing more than playing with math", there are a therefore also actions in Nintex Workflow that can be used for mathematics options. This section is about the operational actions that are available in Nintex Workflow.

Math operation

With the Math operation users can perform basic calculations in their workflow.
The mathematical operations are:

Math operation

- Plus
- Minus
- Divided by
- Multiplied by
- Modulus.

The values that can be used to perform the operations can be static values or dynamic ones.

Build string

The **Build string** can be used to build a new basic string from the available dynamic values or handcrafted data. An example where you would use a **Build string** for is the creation of a URL under the current site;

> One part could be the current site variable {Common:WebUrl}
>
> A hard coded slash /
>
> A Sitename variable {Variable:SiteName}

Regular expression

A regular expression is a sequence of characters that forms a search pattern, mainly for use in matching of strings in "find and replace"-like operations. This action looks like the inline-functions **fn-Remove**, **fn-Replace** and **fn-SubString**.
The action can be used for the following options:

- Checking if a part exists in the text, resulting in a Yes/No result
- Replacement of a part in the text
- Split the text on that part in a collection variable
- Extract from the collection variable the matching strings and stores these in a variable.

A few times we used the **regular expression** action to extract the username from the domain in a NT Domain query like "DOMAIN\Username". Working with regular expression can be very complicated in the beginning; use online test applications or software like Expresso.

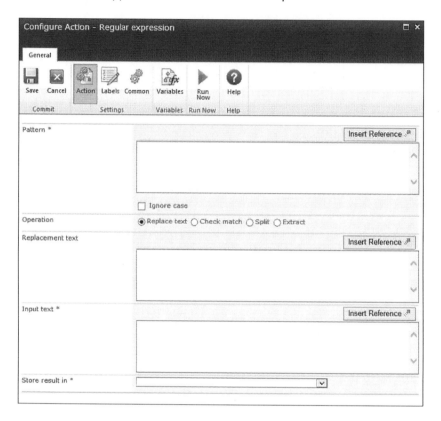

Convert value

The **Convert value** action is used for the conversion of a text variable into another variable type for future use in the current workflow.

Pause for...

This workflow action will pause the workflow for a predefined period of time.
There can be a time set from minutes to years, where you can select the option to use this only during business hours.
Setting a workflow to wait for a few years is maybe not the best option, it's maybe better to schedule a workflow to run every year or so.
If you set the workflow to pause for 1 minute remember that this is not a "real" minute

but more a scheduled minute. As the workflow runs via a timer service the exact time it will take to run the minute can vary from that one minute upto 12 minutes in an over consumed environment.

Pause until...

The **Pause until**... action lets the current workflow pause at this step until the set date and time is reached. The date and time can be set by hand or by a variable. An example where you can use this action is if a user starts a workflow with a start date variable. The variable is used in the **Pause until**... action.

Store Data

One of the great things about IT is maybe that when there is a rule there is also a way to work around that rule. How would that be in relation to traffic? "Yes you are correct when you approach from the right I have to give you priority, but not if it is a Thursday". So we mentioned earlier that a variable only resided in the current running workflow and it ceases to exist when the workflow is ended. With the Store data you can store a workflow variables value so other workflows can use later on.

Retrieve data

The data you set at the Store data action can be read with the Retrieve data action. Via these two actions it's therefore possible to pass variables between two workflow instances.

Schedule

The ability to schedule workflows to run on a specific time is another feature of Nintex Workflow that is very useful. This feature is not available in SharePoint Designer or Visual Studio workflows. In fact, if you want to schedule workflows using SharePoint Designer or Visual Studio, you first need to create a custom timer job to trigger these workflows. Nintex has done that for you and created a customizable and powerful schedule tool, allowing you to set up one-time scheduling as well as repeated scheduling, either per hour, day, or month.

So if you have a workflow that is very server intensive you can schedule it to run on an off peak time and save yourself complaints about the performance issues of your farm.

Snippets

Nintex Workflow has another powerful feature that both Visual Studio and SharePoint Designer lack: Snippets. In Nintex Workflow you can define snippets consisting of several tasks and apply those snippets repeatedly in several workflows. This allows organizations to create complex tasks and then reuse those complex tasks as though they were a single activity. You could for instance save an approval process as approval snippet and reuse this in all your workflows in the current Site Collection.

We saw that with an **Action Set** action you can create snippets. You can also use the Save option and then choose for **Save As Snippet**.

Templates

You can create workflow templates, which are complete workflows that are exportable and reusable not only across sites and site collections but also across entire farms.

The Nintex Workflow templates provide the ability to create complete workflows in an authoring environment, test them in a test environment and then deploy those workflows into the production environment.

Of course, this also means you can test and debug workflows outside the production environment, something with SharePoint Designer is complicated. And since the templates are also exportable, you can keep them in a separate document library to give you the power of document libraries, such as versioning, approval, and backup.

When you have created your workflow just choose save followed by the "Save As Template" option

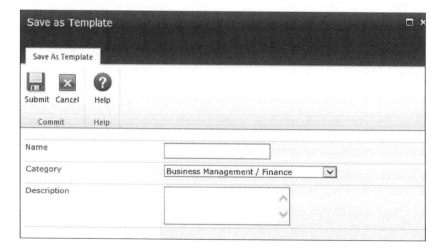

Every time you create a new workflow you are presented with templates so what's more cool than to see your own templates here?

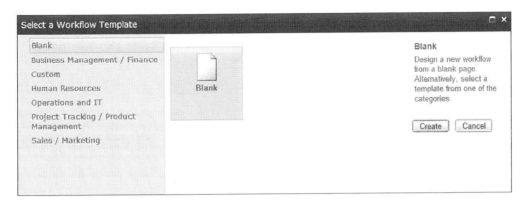

Hands-on: Create a license expiration workflow

In this hands-on we are going to create a workflow for sending reminders if the license for a product is going to expire. The workflow is running every week via a scheduled workflow task and queries the list for the expiration date.

Because we don't want old software to appear in the list there is also a column named Running version.

Create a List

For the purpose of this workflow, a SharePoint list must be created. Ensure that suitable columns are available in the SharePoint list. These are data fields that will be used in the workflow. In this hands-on we will need:

- **Title**, Single line of text field
- **Expiration Date**, date and time field
- **Description**, Multiple lines of text field
- **Running Version**, Yes/No field.

Add items

Add a few items to the list for testing, some are about to expire this month, some are not the latest version and some have the correct date and version.

Create workflow

Now we are going to create expiration workflow.

1. Browse to the Nintex Workflow gallery where you want to create the workflow and select **Create**.

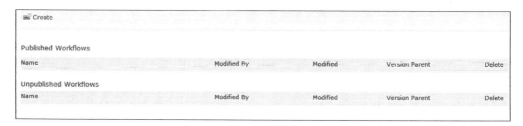

2. Create the following Variables.
   a. TodayNextMonthDate, date and time variable
   b. QueryListCollection, collection variable
   c. ListItemText, text variable
   d. ListItemTextList, text variable.
3. Search for the **Calculate date** action and drag in on the canvas.
4. Configure the action as followed,
   a. **Date field**, check the box **Use date when action is executed**
   b. Set the **Month** field to **1**
   c. Set **Store date** in field to the variable **TodayNextMonthDate**.

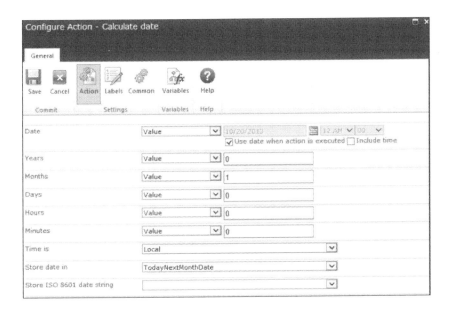

5. Add an **Query list** action and configure this.

6. Select at the List field for **Software List** and expand the **Filter** section.

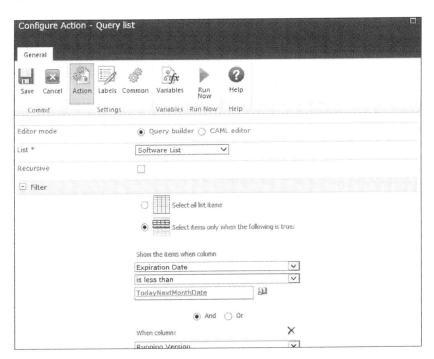

7. Set the **Select items only when the following is true**.
8. Select form the column list the **Expiration Date**.
9. Select **is less than** and **TodayNextMonthDate**.
10. You can also add an filter on the runningversions by clicking the **And** button.
11. Select **Running Version** with the options **Is equal to** and **1**.
    (Yes is 1 in a query and No is 0).
12. From the Field section select **ID** and click on **Add**, you know have selected that you want to retrieve the ID from the list.
13. Set the **ID** section to **QueryListCollection**.

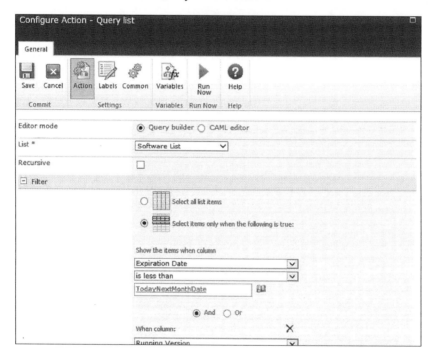

14. Click on **Save** to save the configuration.
15. Add an **For each** action and configure it as follows.
    a. Set Target collection field to **QueryListCollection**
    b. Store result in **ListItemText**
    c. Click on **Save**.

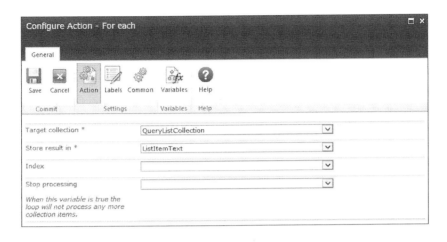

16. Add the **Build string** action to the workflow, this action is used to reconfigure workflow data.

In this Hands-on we are going to use a trick that isn't possible in most workflow applications. We are going to build a list with all the single variables (ListItemText) we received from the **Query List** action and set this into one variable (ListItemTextList).

17. Click in the text field on the **Insert Reference** and add the **ListItemText** from the Workflow Variables Tab, Click **OK**.
18. Set the cursor behind the **{WorkflowVariable:ListItemText}** text and hit **Enter**.
19. Open the **Insert Reference** and add the **ListItemTextList** from the Workflow Variables Tab, Click **OK**.
20. Set the **Store result in** field to **ListItemTextList**.
21. **Save** the action.

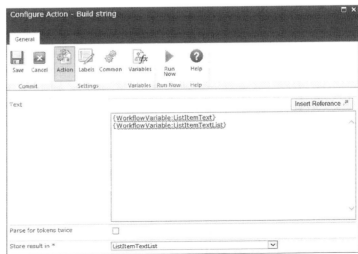

22. Drag a **Send notification** to the last grey block, outside of the **For each** box.
23. Set the **To** field to your account and fill the **Subject**.
24. Add an text and add via the **Insert Reference** the **ListItemTextList** variable. **Save** the action.

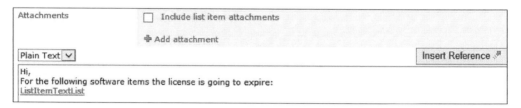

25. Your workflow will now look like the workflow below.
26. **Publish** this workflow and start it on an item in the Software List.

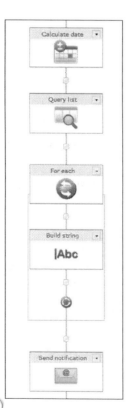

You now receive an e-mail with all items that are going to expire in the coming month.

Advanced Hands-on: Extra leave request options

In the chapter **Simple Workflows** you have created a leave request workflow.

Open this workflow and add the following options into the workflow.

- If the leave request type is sickness no item is created in the calendar due to privacy of the employees (use the **Set a condition** or **Run if** action).

Advanced Hands-on: Bazaar workflow

Many organizations have a place on their intranet where users can sell products that they don't use anymore to their colleagues.

Create a Bazaar list and a workflow for this list with the following options:

- Items created more than a month ago that aren't sold need to be removed from the list to prevent the list from using too much space
- Items that are sold need to be removed after a week
- All items need to be approved before publication as the company needs to prevent the distribution of illegal material via company equipment.

Summary

6 • Creating advanced workflows

In this chapter we've looked at more advanced workflows. What do you need to do when you want to let the workflow decide between going left or right? The "Set a condition", "Run if" and the "For each" are actions that let you make these decisions. We have looked at the operational actions to manipulate variables and use mathematic actions. We used scheduling to run your workflows on off-peak hours.

Saving your workflows as templates and snippets were part of this chapter and can be a real time saver when you often need to reproduce your workflows.

The Hands-on in basic can be used for a lot more examples:

- Create an IT borrowing list for beamers and laptops where the loaner receives a message when the equipment needs to be returned;
- Holiday calendar, send a message a few days in advance to the user to configure the Nintex Task delegation option
- Give the Project Manager a weekly overview of all tasks in his mailbox as a reminder
- And so on...

Also in the Hands-on was the "Build string" action, which we mostly use to reconfigure strings by the inline functions or adding hardcoded text in a dynamic string.

7 • Working with external sources

All the workflows that we have created so far had the data source that was used in the workflow on the same site or the data was entered by the user. But what if the data for the workflow is from another SharePoint site or from another system; what as the data needs to come from an ERP application?

If you're going to force your users to repeatedly enter the same information every time they start a workflow they aren't going to adopt to using your workflows. Why not let your workflow retrieve the information for the users and help them this way by reducing the possibilities of manual errors and duplicated work.

Considerations when working with external sources

When you work with integrating external resources or LOB (Line of Business) applications in your workflow you have to take a few points into account:

- Additional account for accessing the external system
- Structure of the external application
- Secure communication between applications
- The performance of the external system
- What if the external system is unavailable
- Enterprise license may be required
- Licensing for accessing the external system.

Access account for external system

What kind of access method are you going to use to have your users retrieve data from the LOB application? All "external" actions require a username and password to be set in the action itself; you have several options here:

1. Add the username / password directly in the workflow. This is not recommended; if the password changes all workflows need to be updated with the new password.
2. Create a constant for the username and password. It's a best practice to use for every application, environment and unique permission another username and password.

3. Execute SQL can have the username and password in the connection string but this isn't desirable. If the workflow is downloaded the username password are in plain text viewable and this can therefore become a security risk

At the moment Nintex Workflow doesn't work with SharePoint Secure Store Service, otherwise this would also be a good option. When this will be supported is at the moment unknown.

Structure of the external application

SharePoint isn't the only application out there that uses workflows to automate tasks; there are many software systems like ERP's and CRM's that use this approach.
You have to take into account that when a SharePoint workflow is entering or modifying data in another application this may start a workflow in that application to process your data. This can result in workflows that could crash or workflow that get in a loop.

If you are working with data exchange between systems that interact via workflows you need to establish on forehand the best approach and the best application for interaction with this data.
We love to use SharePoint workflows for almost everything in our organization, but there are times that it is better to keep the data in the preferred application and only retrieve the data to SharePoint.

Secure communication

When sending and receiving data from other system via web services, on or off premise but also with cloud solutions, you need to be sure that the communication is secured. Only use services and systems from companies that are trusted by your company and use HTTPS SSL to connect to them.
Let your system administrator add the certificate change to the SharePoint farm trust to prevent errors when calling the HTTPS site

Performance of the external system

When retrieving information from an external application you also have an impact on the system performance of that external application. Is that application sized for the extra data request you are performing? When a Nintex Workflow is executed the actions are executed one after the other without delay. If the external application doesn't respond in timely fashion the workflow will continue without the retrieved data and most likely will break the workflow. You can add "Pause for" actions in your workflow to overcome this issue. Also a question to ask is if it's wise to use Nintex for executing tasks on the external system when thinking about performance; a Nintex for each loop that calls a SQL query is never faster than a SSIS solution due to ETL (http://en.wikipedia.org/wiki/Extract,_transform,_load)

External system is unavailable

What is worse than a system that isn't performing? A system that is down!
When adding information from other applications into your own you also have to think what's going to happen when that application has become unavailable. Always limit your dependency from other systems: "as they break, your application will also break".
As we stated earlier, we don't want to let the users enter duplicate content. So you need to build an application that continues to work when another system is not available.

Use the "Error handling" option in the actions to let the workflow carry on as without the "Error handling" the workflow crashes directly. You can check if the "Error handling" variable is set and then stop the workflow properly.
If the external application is connected via a BCS connection with SharePoint you could also try the "Execute Search" action. The Search service uses his cached data (index) when you perform a search query; this might just be enough for your workflow.
Let the external application be crawled via the BCS connector.

Enterprise license

When you are going to use a connection to an external resource, you are almost always going to have the Enterprise version of Nintex Workflow. There is one exception and thankfully it's the most used integration action; the "Call web service" action is also available with Nintex Workflow Standard. When you want to use other integration options like SQL, BCS, AD or BizTalk you are going to need Nintex Workflow Enterprise. SharePoint is also available in more license types. When you want to use Excel Services or Access Services to connect to the external application you need to have the Enterprise version of SharePoint.

Licensing for accessing external system

Along with most people out there we are also thinking of the cost of application and how we can reduce this. Most application use a licensing model where you have to pay for the amount of users that work with that application or access the data from the application. When accessing the data from an application via a web service or BCS connection via one user account it seems that you only have to purchase one user license. Be aware that via the license agreement it may be forbidden to use a singe account for data access, and that for every user working with the retrieved data an license is required.

Some applications, like SharePoint, deny the use of SQL queries against the SharePoint databases and will set you in an unsupported mode as stated by Microsoft below:

Read Operations Addendum
Reading from the SharePoint databases programmatically, or manually, can cause unexpected locking within Microsoft SQL Server which can adversely affect performance. Any read operations against the SharePoint databases that originate from queries, scripts, .dll files (and so on) that are not provided by the Microsoft SharePoint Development Team or by Microsoft SharePoint Support will be considered unsupported if they are identified as a barrier to the resolution of a Microsoft support engagement.

Call Web Services from a workflow

The **Call a web service** action is the most used method of retrieving information from other applications and uses xml messages send by SOAP requests. Most applications used today and also Share-Point itself uses web services to interact with other applications.

> **To retrieve data from salesforce.com into SharePoint you could use the "Call a web service"**

You remember when we said that you can't connect to data outside of the current site and that the site is the boundary for information? Well with the **Call a web service** action you can retrieve information from everywhere in your SharePoint environment and use it in your workflow. Perfect you might think, but the catch is that using web services is more complex than the **Query list** action.

Connect to web service

First set the URL field with the web service you want to connect to. See the list further in this section of the available web services in SharePoint, for now we use the lists web service. The URL is built up from default URL added with `/_vti_bin/lists.asmx` for example the URL to connect to the web service from our environment called http://intranet would be

```
http://intranet/_vti_bin/lists.asmx
```

In a production environment you would use the Insert Reference function Web URL to use a dynamic connection

```
Web URL/_vti_bin/lists.asmx
```

Add the username and Password you want to connect with, using a Constants for this is always a good practice. Now click the **Refresh** button next to Web method to retrieve the available web methods from the web service.

Web service Input

When you are connecting to a SharePoint web service and select a web method from the pull-down, Nintex Workflow automatic updates the "Web service input" fields when you are in SOAP builder mode with the required information fields.

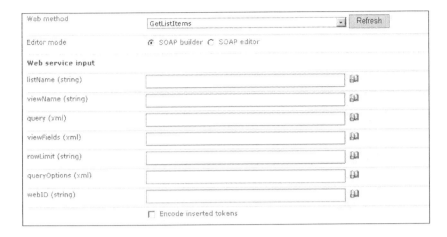

In the image above we have chosen for the "GetListItems" web method and the required "Web service input" fields are displayed. This way Nintex made it easier for you to be sure that all fields are correctly filled. All "Web service input" fields have an address book where you can select workflow data like variables and inline functions.

If you are connecting to other applications or have selected the SOAP editor option you will need to create the xml message yourself via the SOAP editor. If the web service method requires complex parameters you also need to use the SOAP Editor.

Web service Output

The result received by the web service is by default a simple string. There are several methods in Nintex Workflow to process the result.

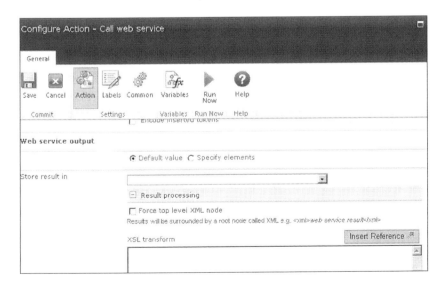

Default value

With the default value the entire string is saved to a text variable which is modifiable with the following options

- Force top level XML node: the results will be surrounded by a root node called XML e.g. <xml>web service result</xml> .
  This is useful if the result from the web service is not XML or is an XML fragment with no root node.
- XSL Transform: An XSL template can be used to transform the results.
  This transform will be applied to the web service results before they are stored in the workflow variable.

Specify elements

You can select one or more elements from the web service results with the "Specify Elements" option. Click on the **Select Element** button to open a XML Browser and click on the required element, then click on **Apply**. Repeat this for all the required elements in the XML Browser.

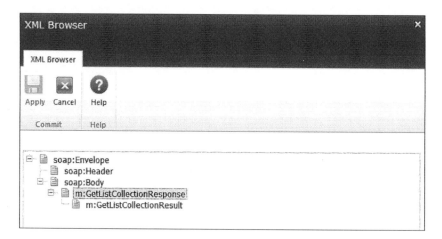

The selected elements are now available within the **Call Web Service** action and you can add a Workflows Variables to them.

Error Handling

There is an error handling option in mostly all external connections actions and that isn't there for show. When working with these actions you must be aware that the external application can be unavailable. If this is the case the web service will retrieve an error and the workflow crashes; the workflow will display the message Error Occurred. In the Workflow History the error message is displayed stating what caused the workflow to crash.

When enabling the Error handling by settings the Capture errors to yes, the workflow will continue to run in case it receives an error from the current action. Two variables also need to be created for the error messaging, one variable from the type Yes/No and one from the type text.

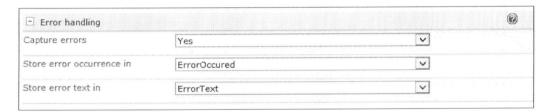

In the design phase of your workflow you can add a **Run if** action that will send an e-mail to you when the Yes/No variable (in the image above the ErrorOccured) is set to yes. That way you receive an e-mail when the workflow receives an error.

Available web services
The following list of web services are available in SharePoint

Friendly Name	Location	Description
Alerts	/_vti_bin/alerts.asmx	Provides methods for working with alerts for list items in a SharePoint site.
Authentication Web service	/_vti_bin/Authentication.asmx	Provides ability for Web services to operate in conjunction with forms authentication.
BDC Web service	/_vti_bin/businessdatacatalog.asmx	Business Data Catalog metadata Web service. Reserved for internal use only.
Copy Web service	/_vti_bin/Copy.asmx	Provides methods for copying items between locations in the SharePoint environment.
List Data Retrieval Web service	/_vti_bin/DspSts.asmx	Provides a method for performing queries against lists in Windows SharePoint Services.
Document Workspace Web service	/_vti_bin/DWS.asmx	Provides methods for managing Document Workspace sites and the data they contain.
Excel Services Web service	/_vti_bin/ExcelService.asmx	Provides methods to call Excel Services remotely or to work as a callback for Web Parts.
Forms Web service	/_vti_bin/Forms.asmx	Provides methods for returning forms used in the user interface when working with the contents of a list.
Forms Services proxy Web service	/_vti_bin/FormsServiceProxy.asmx	Provides methods for Forms Services to proxy requests to remote data sources from Web-based forms.
Forms Services Web service	/_vti_bin/FormsServices.asmx	Provides methods to call Forms Services remotely or to work as a callback for Web-based forms.
Imaging Web service	/_vti_bin/Imaging.asmx	Provides methods that enable you to create and manage picture libraries.
Lists Web service	/_vti_bin/Lists.asmx	Provides methods for working with lists and list data.
Meetings Web service	/_vti_bin/Meetings.asmx	Provides methods that enable you to create and manage Meeting Workspace sites.
Official File Web service	/_vti_bin/officialfile.asmx	Provides methods for sending files to a records repository.
People Web service	/_vti_bin/People.asmx	Provides methods for working with security groups.
Permissions Web service	/_vti_bin/Permissions.asmx	Provides methods for working with the permissions for a site or list.

7 • Working with external sources

Friendly Name	Location	Description
Published Links Web service	/_vti_bin/publishedlinksservice.asmx	Office system client applications and other applications can obtain the list of published links on the server that are targeted to the current user.
Publishing Service Web service	/_vti_bin/PublishingService.asmx	Provides methods to remotely work with the publishing service.
Search Web service	/_vti_bin/search.asmx	Allows access to Enterprise Search results from client applications and Web applications outside of the context of a SharePoint site.
SharePoint Directory Management Web service	/_vti_bin/sharepointe-mailws.asmx	Provides methods for remotely managing distribution groups.
Sites Web service	/_vti_bin/sites.asmx	Provides methods for returning information about the site templates for a site collection.
Slide Library Web service	/_vti_bin/SlideLibrary.asmx	Provides methods for slide library call-backs or remote publishing of slides.
Search Crawl Web service	/_vti_bin/spscrawl.asmx	Provides methods for remote Office SharePoint Server 2007 server farms to crawl a local farm.
Search Web service	/_vti_bin/spsearch.asmx	Provides methods for remotely performing searches within a Windows SharePoint Services deployment.
Users and Groups Web service	/_vti_bin/UserGroup.asmx	Provides methods for working with users, site groups, and cross-site groups.
User Profile Change Web service	/_vti_bin/userprofilechangeservice.asmx	Provides methods to query the user profiles change log remotely.
User Profile Web service	/_vti_bin/userprofileservice.asmx	Provides a user profile interface for remote clients.
Versions Web service	/_vti_bin/versions.asmx	Provides methods for working with file versions.
Views Web service	/_vti_bin/Views.asmx	Provides methods for working with views of lists.
Web Part Pages Web service	/_vti_bin/webpartpages.asmx	Provides the methods to send information to and retrieve information from Web services.
Webs Web service	/_vti_bin/Webs.asmx	Provides methods for working with sites and subsites.
Workflow Web service	/_vti_bin/workflow.asmx	Provides methods to work with workflows.

Using Execute SQL

When you want to retrieve and store information directly into a database you can use the "Execute SQL" action. Remember that it's not allowed to connect directly to the SharePoint databases to store data that way.

At the minimum the following fields are required: the connection string to the database, and the query that you want execute at the database.

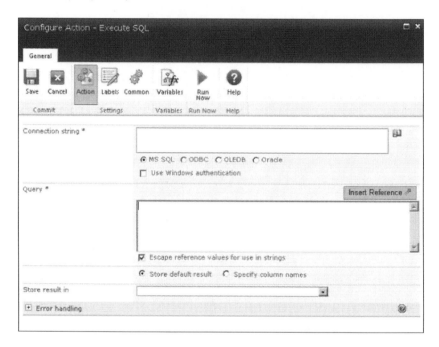

Connection String

In the connection string you provide the information to create a connection to the server and the required database. If SQL authentication is required also set User ID and Password. For example:

```
Data Source=myServerAddress;Initial Catalog=myDataBase;Integrated
Security=SSPI;
```

Beneath the connection string there are four data providers; a data provider is used for connecting to a database, executing commands, and retrieving the results. The providers are the SQL provider, ODBC provider, OleDB provider and the Oracle provider.

Use windows authentication

By selecting **Use Windows Authentication** the connection to the database will be made using integrated authentication. This enables the "Credentials" fields where a username and password or a Nintex Constant can be entered. This username or constant needs to have sufficient database permissions to retrieve the data from database.

Query

This is where the query is configured that needs to be executed against the database, the data can be entered directly or via the Insert Reference option. As most of us out there aren't full blooded DBA administrators it's best to first check your query in SQL server management studio or use the Run Now from the Action's navigation. Saving and Publishing your workflow for every single query practice won't help speeding up in the workflow build.

The "Escape reference values for use in strings" option is to ensure that values from the Insert Reference option is escaped to use in a SQL string. If the SQL statement is a single variable this option needs to be unchecked.

Store result in

The **Store result in** lets you define how the results from the SQL query are stored, there are here two options:

- "Store default result" contains all the workflow variables that can be used to store the result of a SQL query. A collection variable can be used to store multiple records. If a variable that is not a collection is selected, only the first record will be stored. If multiple columns are returned, only the value of the first column will be stored.
- "Specify column name" is used to store the query result from a column name that is returned by the SQL query.

Error Handling

As in the **Call Web Service** action there is also in the Execute SQL action an Error Handling option that is very helpful when creating a workflow for troubleshooting and later when the workflow is in production to prevent the workflow from crashing.

Query BCS

Query BCS is an action used to retrieve data from Business Connectivity Services. If you are working with SharePoint 2007 this was then called the Business Data Catalog (BDC) in MOSS 2007.

With SharePoint Designer or Visual Studio the connection to the external data is created and saved: the Query BCS can then use this BCS applications.

The combined SAP / Microsoft application Duet Enterprise also uses the BCS applications model to retrieve data from SAP into SharePoint. If required the Query BCS could then be used to get to the SAP data. For more information about Duet Enterprise have a look at http://bit.ly/1cVYIdZ

The options in "Query BCS" are almost identical to these from the actions "Call Web Service" and "Execute SQL". In the first part you are asked which Credentials are used when connecting to the BCS application. This account needs to have execute permissions on the BCS Model and of course permissions in the external application.

The application name is a pull down list containing all BCS applications that are available at the current SharePoint environment. After selecting the Application name the available instances within that application can be selected in the Instance name field.

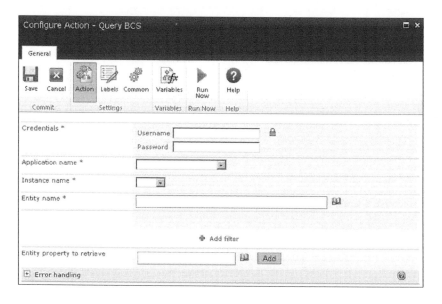

The Entity name is the same as an external content type and can be extended with filters to retrieve the correct information.

The "Entity property to retrieve" field contains the properties in the entity that are queried, several properties can be retrieved at once. For every property there also needs to be a variable created. If a variable that is not a collection is selected, only the first result will be stored.

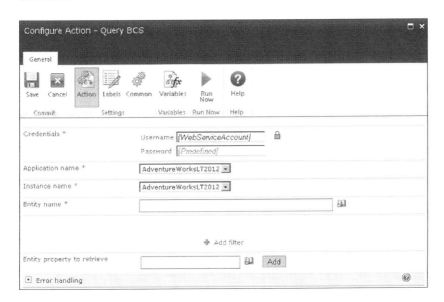

Hands-on: Create a workflow with a SharePoint web service

The following hands-will use a web service to retrieve data from SharePoint

1. Go to the **Site Actions** menu and select **Site Settings**.
2. Select below the **Nintex Workflow** section the **Manage workflow constants** Option.
3. Click **New**.

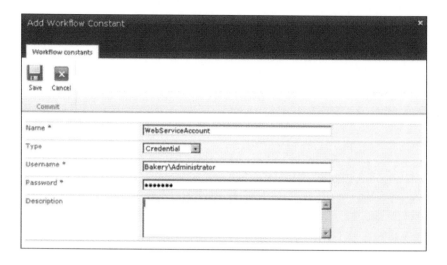

4. Provide a logical name for the constant, we use **WebServiceAccount**.
5. Type is **Credentials** and provide the administrator **Username** and **Password**.
6. Click on **Save**.
7. Return to your library and the workflow settings, click **Manage Workflows with Nintex Workflow**.
8. Click on the **Create** link to create a new workflow.
9. Choose the **Blank Template**.
10. Click in the actions menu on **Integration** and drag the **Call web service** on the canvas.

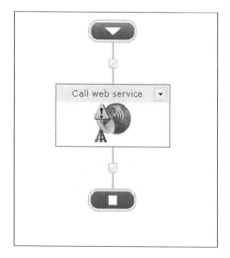

11. Double-click the action to configure it.
12. Click on the address book next to URL.
13. Double-click on **Web URL**, the Web URL appears in the **Dynamic text** to insert.
14. Append the following to the Dynamic text to insert box

    `/_vti_bin/usergroup.asmx`

    so the text is

    `Web URL/_vti_bin/usergroup.asmx`
15. Click **OK**.
16. Click on the lock next tot **Username**, Select **WebServiceAccount** and Click **Insert**.

17. Click on the refresh button to retrieve the **webservices**.
18. Click **OK** on the **URL**.
19. Select from the Web method list the option **GetUserCollectionFromSite**.

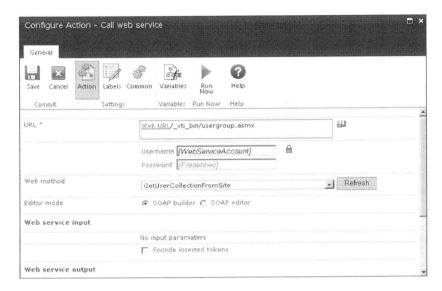

20. We need to store the outcome so click the **Variables** button and select **New**.
21. The Name will be **varWebServiceResult**, Type **Multiple lines of text**.
22. Click **Save** to save the variable and **Close** to return to the workflow.
23. Beneath Web service output in **Store results** in select the newly created variable **varWebServiceResult**.
24. Click **Save** to save the action.
25. **Click in the search box in the Actions** menu and type **log**.

26. Drag the **Log in history list** to the canvas.
27. Double-click on the action to configure it.
28. Click on **Insert Reference** and go to the tab Workflow Variables.
29. Double-click **varWebServiceResult** and click on **OK**.
30. Click on **Save**.

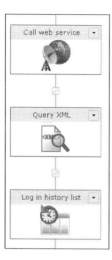

31. Click on **Publish**.
32. Set the Title to **WebService** and click on **Submit**, click on **OK**.
33. Return to the library and start the workflow via item menu and workflows.
34. Select **start a new workflow**.
35. Select the WebService workflow.
36. Click on **Start**.

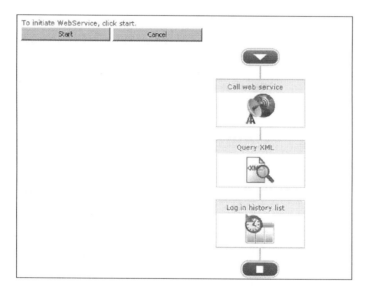

37. You are redirected to the document library and you can see that the workflow is **Completed**.
38. From the item menu select **View Workflow History**.

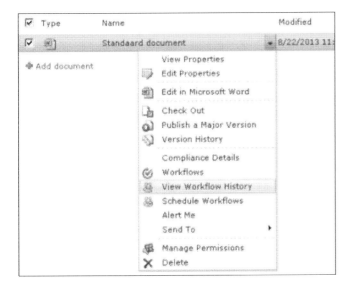

39. Select the workflow **WebService**.

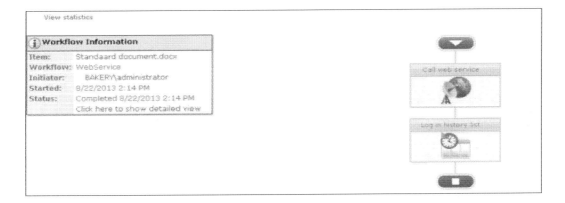

40. Click on the link **Click here to show detailed view**.
41. You see the workflow **Messages part** where in the message the result from the web service call is displayed.

Hands-on: Force an workflow in an error

In this hands-on we are going to force a workflow into an error, as it is better to have an error in practice than in production.

1. Go to the previous created workflow.
2. Open the call Web Service action and click on the **Refresh** button.
3. Click on the **OK** button and select from the Web method list the option **RemoveGroup**.
4. Under the Web service input section there is one input field **groupName (string)**.
5. Enter a group name that you are sure that doesn't exist in your SharePoint environment. In our example we use the fictitious group Parrot.

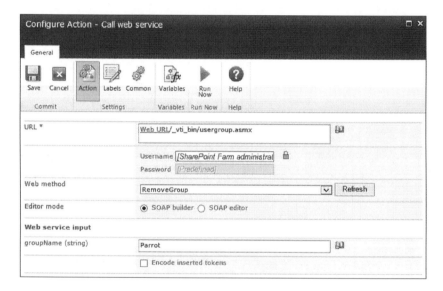

6. Save the modified workflow and publish it.
7. Start the workflow on an item, after the redirection back to the document library and you can see that the workflow displays **Error Occurred**.
8. Click on the **Error Occurred** text to go to the workflow results.

9. Click on the **Terminate this workflow now** text to stop the workflow.

Hands-on: Enable Error logging

The following hands-will enable error logging on a **Call web service** action.

Create Variable

1. Go to library where you've created the workflow from the previous hands-on.
2. Open the previous created workflow.
3. Select from the Top menu section Workflow Settings the option **Variables**.

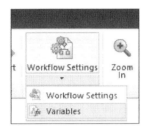

4. Create 2 variables:
   a. Name: **ErrorOccruredYesNo**
      Type: **Yes/No**
   b. Name: **ErrorOccruredText**
      Type: **Single line of text.**
5. Double-click the **Call a webservice** action to configure it.
6. Expand the Error handling section.

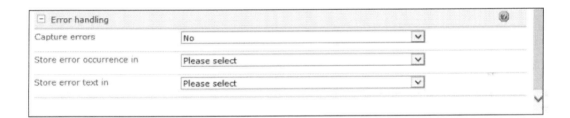

7. Set the Capture errors on **Yes**.
8. Set the field **Store error occurrence in** on the variable **ErrorOccruredYesNo**.
9. Set the field **Store error text in** on the variable **ErrorOccruredText**.
10. Close the action and save the workflow.

If the web service would receive an error the workflow will continue instead of crashing.

Advanced hands-on: Create a list via web service

Try to create a workflow that will make a list on a site using the SharePoint web service `_vti_bin/lists.asmx` and the method AddList.

The 3 required parameters for this method are:

- listName, the name you want to give to the list, it must be a unique name within the current site
- description, a description for the list
- templateID, the type of list you want to create.
  For the hands-on choose the id **100** (Generic list).

By default the list isn't displayed in the left navigation, try to use a web service to do this. (UpdateList as method and the field listproperty <List OnQuickLaunch = True>).

Summary

7 • Working with external sources

In this part of the document we have looked at working with data from other systems. What are the possibilities and what are the pitfalls when using external applications? Is it allowed to connect to the external system via a SQL Query, and what about the licensing model for interacting via web services?
How are you going to react to a system outage or a slow environment are all things to consider when retrieving data from those applications.

We have looked at three methods of retrieving data: via web services, via BCS or via database queries. When working with these actions there are always a few steps that need to be taken:

- Specify the Connection URL or application
- User account used when processing
- Data to query
- Method to retrieve
- Error Handling.

And finally, when working with these actions use Error Handling to save the workflow from crashing.

8 • Almost programming

This section of the book goes a lot deeper into workflows and even goes beyond the normal steps into the functionality you could call programming. As we've told you in the beginning of the book with Nintex Workflow you can create complex workflows without the use of Visual Studio and any developer. But that doesn't have to stop you from creating workflows developers could be proud off.

State machine and sequential workflows

When working with workflows there are two varieties: a sequential workflow or a state machine workflow. The sequential workflow is the simple version and we used this type in all our workflows. A sequential workflow runs in a predefined sequence. We can change the path via the **Set condition** or **Run if** actions but in the end the workflows still run from top to bottom.

A state machine workflow is different and more complex as these types of workflows can go forward and backwards in the current running workflow; they do this via states. Every state can be seen as a small sequential workflow, and the rule that the workflow runs from top to bottom applies to the actions in that state. When the end of the state is reached you can start another state and the actions in that state or stop the workflow. You always need to tell the workflow that it has to stop or the workflow will keep on running indefinitely.

In the picture on the right we have created an example of a state machine workflow. The workflow has three stages with a few actions in every stage. On the last action of each stage we move to the next stage.

Why would you use state machine workflows if they are more complex than sequential workflow? Because a state machine workflow is much more capable of working with human interaction!

State machine example

Let's set out an example: You have created a workflow where the user, his manager and the Security Officer need to approve a security request; so in the workflow there are 3 approval moments. One approval for the user, one for the manager and one for the Security Officer.

> Now we start the workflow and the user approves the request, the manager declines this as he first wanted to know why this request is needed.
> The workflow is restarted and the user and his manager now approve however the Security Officer declines as he thinks that this is a major security issue. The user convinces the Security Officer that the impact is minimal and the change required.
> The workflow is now restarted and all people approve.

In this example the user needed to approve his security request three times before he finally can get his change. If this happens on a daily basis you can image that the users are going to try to work around the system as it isn't efficient.

If we had created a state machine workflow for this scenario we could have let the user approve only one time and the workflow would switch between the approval state of the manager and the Security Officer. The image below shows this exact workflow where the user state is the Initial state, Manager state is the part where the manager approves and the Security Officer state is where the Security Officer approves.

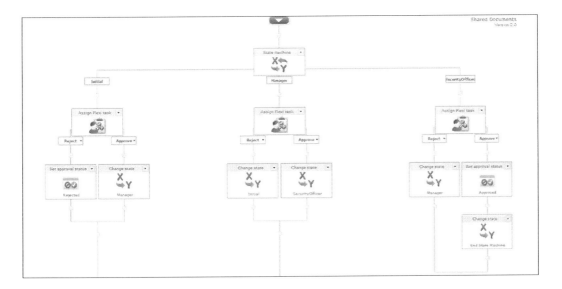

When looking at business processes that you want to automate with workflows you'll see a pattern where you can replace the sequential workflows for state machine workflows.

- A project: the initiation, planning, execution, monitoring and completion phases can be converted to states
- Bug tracking: Record a bug, Analyse it, Assign to a developer, Resolve the bug, Test the resolution and Release the new version are valid states.

Creating a state machine

The state machine workflow requires 2 new actions the **state machine** action and the **change state** action. The **state machine** action is the action where the state machine workflow section runs in. Open the action to configure the states where the workflow consists of; in the image below these are the states Initial, Manager and SecurityOfficer. The initial state, this is the state where the state machine workflow section start from, needs to be selected from the entered states.

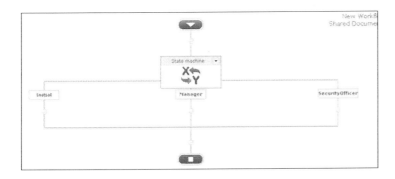

To switch between the different states in the workflow the **Change state** action is used; the states that are available are selectable from a dropdown menu.

A state machine workflow keeps running until the workflow reaches a **Change state** action where the End state machine is configured, so remember to add this to your workflow.

And that is really it, have a look at the Hands-on later where we will create an approval state machine workflow.

Splitting a workflow

When a workflow is getting larger and larger it gets difficult to keep track even with Nintex Workflow, it is complicated to keep an overview of the processes where the workflow is running and adding functionality to that workflow even more of a challenge.

If a workflow gets too big it's best to split the current workflow into two or more workflows to help the maintainability, also if the workflow results in error only a part of the process needs to be restarted instead of the whole workflow.

There is no exact science for when a workflow needs to be split up as there are too much variables to be taken into account. We are going to use a very simple example where we show the theory of splitting so that you can apply this on your own workflows.

We created a workflow where there are 2 approval phases, one for the Manager and if he approves then one for the SEO.

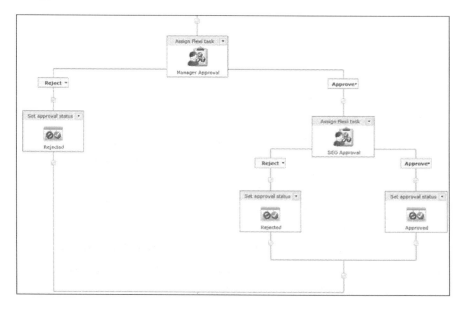

The best place to split this workflow is when the workflow switches from "stage". In our example there are 2 stages: "the manager approval stage" and "the SEO approval stage". After the first stage is completed the second stage directly is started, so the best place would be directly before that second stage.

In the following image we created a new workflow named **Approve CEO** and removed the **Assign flexi task** action that request approval from the SEO by the **Start workflow** action that starts the **Approve CEO** workflow.

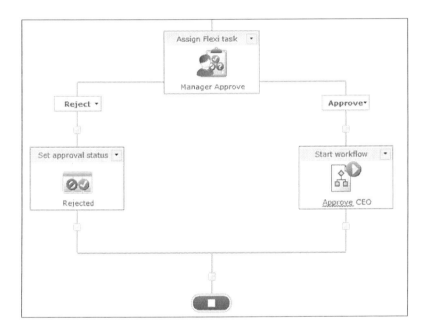

This was an easy example but in most cases it isn't always that simple.

A good practice for splitting your workflow is to keep looking for those "phases" or "stages" in your workflows, as there it's easier to split your workflow.

Avoid splitting up workflows on places in your workflow where there's a lot of interaction with external systems as this makes the workflow complicated if the other system becomes unavailable or reacting slow on user responses.

If you want to pass variables, have a look at the **Store data** and **Retrieve data** actions, we are going to show an example later on.

Also remember that you don't always have to split up a workflow. First have a look at using action sets and state machine functions to bring structure to your workflow. Maybe then you don't have to split up the workflow after all.

Starting a workflow from a workflow

We already used the start workflow action in the previous section. We now are going to look at this and the other options that are available to start a workflow from within a workflow.

Start workflow

The **Start workflow** action can be used to start another workflow from the current list or library, for starting workflows on other lists or sites you use the web service action. The action contains an option to start the workflow immediately or schedule the start. When the **Schedule** option is selected the action adds functions where the start time, the end schedule and the repeating of the workflow can be set.

As with most field values these values can be set by hand of via workflow data.

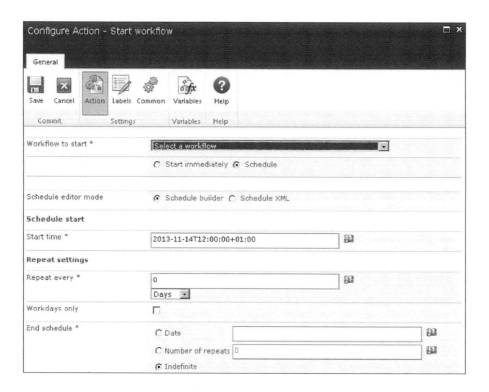

This action doesn't have an option to schedule the start of the workflow after a few minutes or hours; this needs to be created via adding the **Pause for...** action in front of this action.

Starting a workflow via web service

In the previous chapter, **Working with External sources** we have already looked at the web services that are available in SharePoint and how we can use them. When you installed Nintex Workflow you also installed a few Nintex workflow web service functions. With two of the web services methods we can start workflows: **Startworkflow** and **StartworkflowOnListItem**.

Starting a workflow via a web service can be very helpful, for example: you have an extranet environment where you and your customers work together. Every customer represents a site with unique permissions so their customers don't see each other's website. Hopefully for you there a lot of sites.

With the web service function you can start via one single workflow with one service account on all sites a workflow and use that to update information on all these sites. You can even first publish a new workflow on the site of your customers and then start that workflow.

Startworkflow

The web service action can be contacted via the requested URL with `/_vti_bin/NintexWorkflow/workflow.asmx` added to the URL.

It's important to specify the URL where the workflow exists as the web service only can start these workflows.

The **StartWorkflow** method has three input variables from which two are required:

- fileurl field needs to be filled with the complete URL of the item where the workflow will run on and is a required field
- workflowName is the exact name of the workflow and is off course also required
- associationData is used as parameter for entering start data into the workflow and can be used to enter values into variables. This field is not required.

StartworkflowOnListItem

When the name of an item where the workflow needs to run on isn't known or the item is created during the current workflow the **StartWorkflowOnListItem** web method can be used to start a new workflow in that item.

The difference between the two workflow methods is that where the **StartWorkflow** requires the fileurl of the item where the workflow is going to run, the **StartWorkflowOnListItem** requires the **ItemID** and the **listname**.

The **ItemID** could be a list Item ID variable from an item that first is created in the current workflow.

The **workflowName** and the **associationData** are available here, where the **workflowName** again is required.

Variables between workflows

When splitting a workflow into several workflows and when starting a workflow from another workflow you run into the problem that you can't use the current variables.
As you may remember the content of a variable will only run in the current workflow and if the workflow ends so will the variable content.
Luckily there are a few methods to pass along the variables from the current workflow into the next.
In the two previous web service actions we could use the **associationData** option to set start data. This start data then can be used in the workflow as a normal variable.

With the actions **Store data** and **Retrieve data** you can save the variables from the current workflow and retrieve them via the Retrieve data action in another workflow. Both workflows need to be running so it's best to use a **pause for...** action to keep the first workflow available.

So there are options to get variables between workflows, but sometimes it's just easier to save the outcome of a workflow to a hidden field in the current list and get that field into the next workflow. OK, it isn't the nicest method but it works! One thing you mustn't do is combine these methods, as this makes things unnecessarily complicated.

Performance

SharePoint uses a queuing system to control workflow-related stress on farm resources and the content databases, and as Nintex workflow uses the SharePoint workflow service, it has to obey that rule. By using this system, when the number of workflows executing against a database reaches a threshold, successive workflow operations are added to the queue to be run by the Workflow Timer service. When splitting workflows and starting one from another, it's good to keep the performance of the system in mind so your workflows aren't flooding the environment.

Developing actions

What are we going to develop now? No, as I'm not a developer I'm not going to tell you how to develop. What we are going to tell is that if you require a custom action that isn't available, you could develop this yourself or let this be developed for you.

When you have created an account on connect.nintex.com you can go to the downloads section. In the downloads area beneath the Nintex Workflow 2010 Downloads a part about SDK NW2010. Download the **Nintex Workflow 2010 SDK - info and download** and install this on a server where Visual Studio and Nintex is installed.

In the folder C:\Program Files (x86)\Nintex\Nintex Workflow 2010 SDK there are a few examples and tutorials about creating an action, deploying workflows via wsp's and more.

Hands-on: Create a state machine workflow

The following hands-will create a machine state approval workflow. In the example we are going to create a workflow where the user first approves, then his manager needs to approve and the last step is that the Security officer needs to give his approval. As there are no extra accounts we need to use the administrator for approval

1. Start by creating a new blank Nintex Workflow in the library.
2. Click on the Top menu the **Workflow Settings**.
3. Set the **Start when items are created** to **Yes**, click on **Save**.
4. Select from the **Logic and flow** section in the Action Menu for the action **state machine**.
5. Configure the action.
a. Change the name of State 1 to **Initial**
b. Change the name of State 2 to **Manager**
c. Add a new state and name this **SecurityOfficer**.
6. Set the state to start on **Initial.**

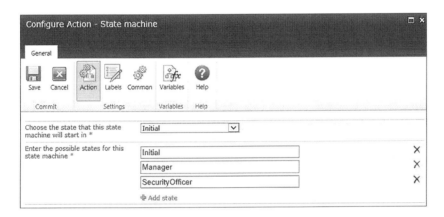

7. **Save** the action.

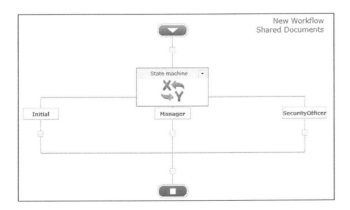

8. Drag from the Actions menu the **Assign Flexi task** to **Initial.**
9. Double-click the action to configure it.

10. Click on the address book, in the Lookup section select the **Initiator** and click on **Add**.
11. Click **Save** for saving the changes to the action.
12. Search in the action menu on the word **State**.
13. Drag the **Change state** to the Approve path.

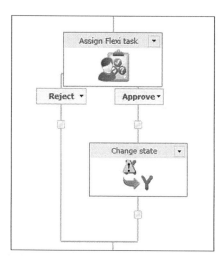

14. Double-click the action and set the **Next state** to **Manager** and click **Save**.
15. Click the **Assign Flexi task** menu and select **Copy**.
16. Go to the **Manager** phase, click the grey box and select **Paste**.
17. Repeat for **SecurityOfficer**.
18. Your workflow will now look like this:

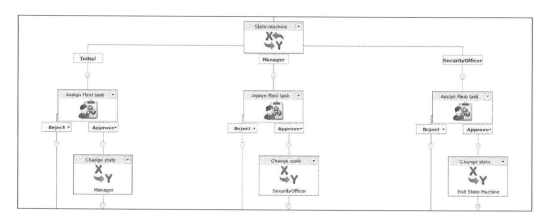

19. Go to the **Manager** phase and the change state beneath **Approve**.
20. Change the Next state to **SecurityOfficer** and click **Save**.
21. Go to the **SecurityOfficer** phase and the change state beneath **Approve**.
22. Change the Next state to **End state machine** and click **Save**.
23. Now we need to change the approvers, double-click the **Assign Flexi task** beneath **Manager**.

24. Remove the **Initiator** and change this to another account.
25. Change the assignee for **SecurityOfficer** also to another account.
26. Drag the **Set approval status** beneath the **Reject** step in the Initial phase.
27. Configure to **action to Rejected.**
28. Drag another **Set approval status** to the far right (beneath **SecurityOfficer**, under **Approve**) above the **Change state.**
29. Set the Action to **Approved.**
30. Your workflow now looks like this:

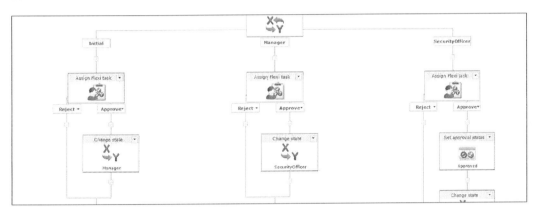

31. The approval steps and the steps forward are now configured, now it's time to configure the steps back.
32. Drag a new **Change state** on the canvas to the **Manager state, Reject.**
33. Configure the state to **Initial** and **Save** the action.
34. Copy the action and paste it at the **SecurityOfficer** state beneath, reject.
35. Configure it so the state changes to **Manager.**
36. The workflow now looks like this:

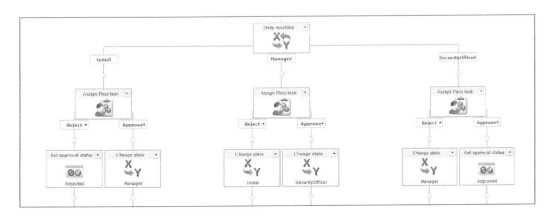

37. Last add a **Change state** to the left under the **Set approval status** and set this to **End state machine**.
38. **Publish** the workflow with the name **StateMachine**.
39. Upload a new document to automatic start the workflow.

	Type	Name	Modified		Modified By	StateMachine
☐				☐		
	📄	Rotterdam Marathon training	12/13/2013 10:38 AM		bakery\administrator	In Progress
	📄	StateMachineDocument	5/23/2014 9:41 AM		bakery\administrator	In Progress

Hands-on: Starting a workflow from another workflow

In this hands-on we will create a workflow that will start another workflow via a web service call.

We will create a parent workflow that queries a list. For every result we retrieve a child workflow will be started on that item. The child workflow will then update a field in the item so that the parent workflow will not retrieve that item again.

Create a List

For the purpose of this workflow, a SharePoint list must be created named **wfCycle**. Ensure that suitable columns are available in the SharePoint list. These are data fields that will be used in the workflow. In this tutorial we will need:

- Title: Single line of text
- Run: Yes/No field set to default value **Yes**.

Creating the Child Workflow

First we create the child workflow, this is workflow being used to log some data to the workflow history list, it then updates the item Run field to No.
The No value will ensure that the workflow doesn't run again on this particular item.
We create the child workflow first which will allow us to reference it when the parent workflow is created.

1. Create a new workflow.
2. Next, add a **Pause for...**, **Log in history list**, and **Update** item action to the workflow designer. The finished workflow will look similar to the following design.

3. Configure the **Pause for...** action so that it's set to 1 minute.
4. Configure the **Log in history list** action with the Insert reference **ItemID**.
5. Configure the Update item action to modify the **Run** column to **No**.
6. Publish the workflow as **wfCycle_log**.

Creating the Parent Workflow

Once the above steps are completed, you can now create your parent workflow.

1. Select the Workflow Settings toolbar button then the **Create a Workflow** in Nintex Workflow drop-down selection.
2. Within the Workflow Designer, select the **Workflow Settings** drop-down then **Variables**.
3. Select **New**, and create a **List Item ID** named **ListItemID** and a collection variable **col_queryResults**.
4. Next, add a **Query list, For each,** and **Call web service** action to the workflow designer.
5. Configure the **Query list** action to query the **wfCycle** list where Run is equal to **1** (which is equal to Yes) storing the ID field in the **col_queryResults** collection variable as shown on the next page.

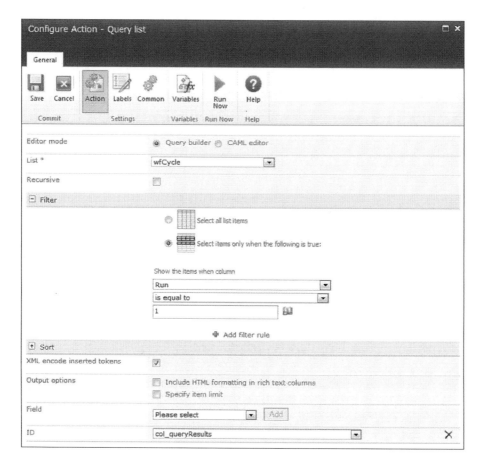

Note: If you already have items within your list where Run is empty or if you want to run the workflow on every item, you can set the Field to List Item ID and remove the filter.

6. Configure the **For each** action which iterates through the **col_queryResults** collection variable, storing each value in the **ListItemID** List Item ID variable which is then used in the Web service call.

7. Next, configure the **Call web service** action using the **StartWorkflowOnListItem** Web method and setting the Web service input fields as shown below.
    Note the following Web service input field descriptions.

• itemId (int) = The **ListItemID** workflow variable you set up above

• listName (string) = The name of the List where the workflow resides

• workflowName (string) = The name of the workflow that you would like to start
   associationData (string) = This can be left blank.

8. **Publish** the workflow as **wfCycle_parent**.

Summary

8 • Almost programming

In this chapter we have seen the state machine workflow. This workflow is in the beginning a little bit complex to understand but if you're familiar with the concept you find yourself creating more state machine workflows then the linear types. The power the state machine workflow has is to jump back and forth when a user rejects or approves which makes these workflows better to react on business processes.

We have now come to the end of our workflow creations: with these last workflows examples we have let you see all basics of creating workflows. As in every company there are many more opportunities that can use a workflow, so go out and find that process that can be helped with a little Nintex automation.

9 • Other functions

The last chapters were all about workflows, in this chapter we are going to look at the additional options as Nintex Workflow has more to offer than only workflow functions.
If you are not yet convinced of the value of Nintex Workflow maybe the following functions can pull you to the dark force, uhh Nintex camp.

LazyApproval

LazyApproval is a great function that really helps the user adoption for working with workflows and SharePoint.
With LazyApproval the user can respond to workflow tasks by directly replying with received e-mail. Is that cool or what?
So a manager receives via an e-mail the message that a workflow task is awaiting his approval on SharePoint. Instead of browsing to the location he just hits the reply button and enters Approve. That's enough to approve the workflow!

To setup LazyApproval there are a few options that need to be configured first on your SharePoint environment:

*   Your need to allow **incoming e-mail** into your SharePoint. This can be a no-go for a system administrator with the argument that they then would receive spam in SharePoint. If they setup SharePoint to only receive e-mails from a safe e-mail server this can be an Exchange server with spam filtering to prevent the server from flooding with unsolicited e-mail
*   Set the **outgoing e-mail,** set the reply address to the address that is going to be used by LazyApproval so the users just can hit reply to approve
*   Than enable LazyApproval and use the same e-mail address as used in the above section
*   Check the **approval and denial terms,** on site collection level or in the Central administration for global configuration. We have a few Dutch customers so we added Dutch approval words to the list
*   Setup the **Phrases to ignore** list if there are more phrases than just the standard "Out of Office".

Nintex Live

Nintex Live is an online catalog where actions can be downloaded from to use in your local SharePoint environment. In Office 365 version of Nintex Workflow the Nintex Live functions are already enabled.

The Nintex Live actions are divided into several categories:
- Communication; e-mail verification and single or bulk text messaging
- Converts & tools; interaction with online save locations as DropBox and Box, Exchange online and for large organization even the option to work with cloud servers
- Finance; live exchange rate and currency converters
- Reference; get ip-address of a web server, the weather forecast and driving directions
- SharePoint; Actions that make it possible to interact with Office365
- Social functions; Facebook, LinkedIn, Twitter and Yammer. Actions to create messages and groups.

In the upcoming periods the amount of available Live action will continue to grow and will support more Cloud services and integration scenarios.

You could use the Nintex Live actions for example in an online marketing process. A user creates a new product page on your internal SharePoint site. After the page is approved the page is converted to an external blog post with the WordPress action. The link to the blog post is then shared via the first social action, Twitter, for example. After a delay of a few hours the page is posted by other social actions.

Working

Nintex Live is a hosted service platform built on Microsoft Azure that connects the service provider (StrikeIron, Twitter, etc) via Web service API's on the one hand side to the customer (Your) environment on the other hand side.
The cloud solution contains a service catalog containing all available web services and a queue management layer used for priority and in case of unavailability of the web service.

Nintex Live requires the Nintex Live framework (nintexlivecore.wsp) installed on the Central Administration server. The framework provides all the common settings and certificates for a secure connection to the Nintex Live network.

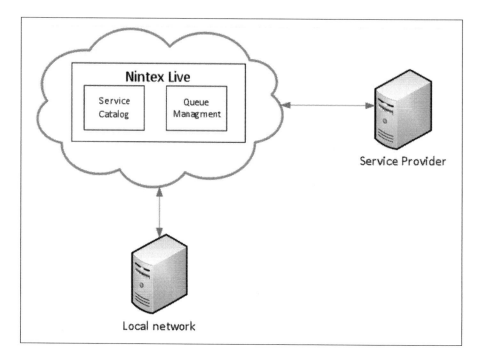

Picture: Working of Nintex Live

Security

Nintex Live uses a key called the Nintex Live ID to identify the customer and doesn't expose the ID of the SharePoint environment to the service provider. Instead when a Nintex Live action is executed, this action gets a randomly generated ID that is internally mapped to the Nintex Live ID of the customer. Via this construction the identity of the requestor is more secure.

The security of the services that you use (Twitter, Facebook, etc) are enforced by first requiring approval for accessing the account on your behalf.
The user needs to login to the service and confirm the usage of the account. You have the option to save the approval in Nintex. If the workflow is restarted Nintex doesn't require the approval again.

NINTEX LIVE

Nintex Live is requesting access to your Twitter account to post the following status:

　　Test from Nintex Workflow

Note: Please ensure that you are not signed in to any existing or previous Twitter sessions in your browser before proceeding.

To proceed to the Twitter website to complete the authorization process, click here.

To deny authorization, click here.

This is an automated email. Do not reply to this email. For support or general inquiries, please email support@nintex.com.

notification@nintexlive.com No Items

Backup

As the Nintex Live ID is a unique ID for using Nintex Live it's advisable to backup this key or save it in a secure location. In case of a catastrophic crash that requires a rebuild of the farm the Nintex Live ID is required to get the correct settings from the Nintex Live network.

Pricing

Nintex Live requires software Assurance for activation.

Be advised that some actions in Nintex Live can contain a license fee. The actions from StrikeIron are on a trial basis for a period of 30 days, after which they will be licensed. Creating or enabling servers from Rackspace and Amazon will be charged to your account at these companies.

Holidays

What is better than going on a holiday? Going on a holiday and work just goes on without you! We have seen that there are several actions that require approval or information from a user to continue the workflow. If the user doesn't respond we can escalate this with the escalations options. The user can prevent the waiting by setting their Holidays.

There are actions that have the option to run only during business days, that way an action that has a delay for 3 days will wait in the weekend and continue the next business day.

But what if there's a holiday? As Nintex Workflow doesn't know if the current company follows the holidays this needs to be set by hand.

There is no direct link to the Farm holidays page. Use therefor the following http://<CentralAdmin>/_layouts/NintexWorkflow/ManageHolidayDates.aspx?Scope=farm

As with most options in Nintex Workflow you can also set the holidays on several levels: Farm level, Site Collection level and Site level. The Farm level could for example be used for setting the global holidays as New Year's day and Christmas for the whole organization; on site collection level the local holidays as the Fourth of July for USA, King's day in the Netherlands and Golden Week in Japan.

Setting holidays can only be done per day, so for a holiday week you need to do this 5 times. The holidays have a repeat function that works on a date basis; so the first of January is valid but the third Tuesday in September needs to be added every year by hand.

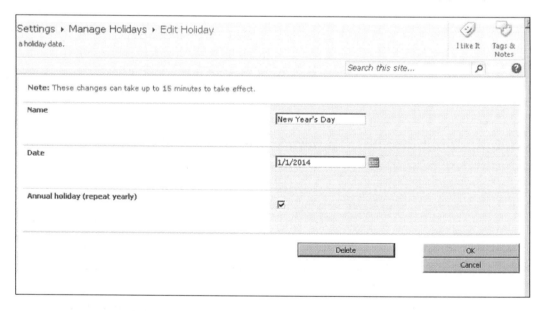

An even better option for using holidays is that users can create their own holidays by going to the personal actions menu and selecting the Nintex Workflow 20**, Task Delegation menu option.

Luckily in this option the user does have the possibility to set a begin and end date for his holiday and select the person to delegate his tasks too. There is also the option to use a Scope for this teamsite only that could be used when the user wants to delegate approvals to another person on this site only.

Message Templates

Nintex Workflows has 2 default message templates build in that are used when sending approval requests to users, the **Approval Required Notification** and the **Approval No Longer Required Notification**.

The layout of these templates can again like most option be changed on the three available levels: farm, site collection and site. How cool would it be that you send the request information to your users in their own department color and logos.

With the sections **Notification Header** and **Notification Footer** the top and bottom of the send messages can be changed from the now orange bar to a color representing the company layout.

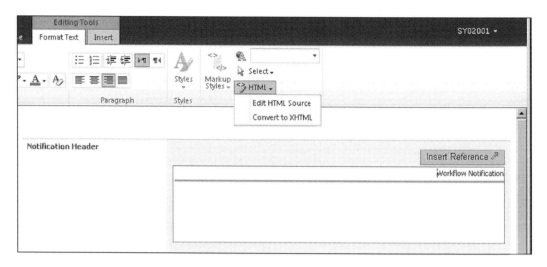

If the workflow designer needs the option to Enforce message header and footer this option can be set in the Global Settings of Nintex workflow.

Reporting

In one of the first chapters (Simple workflows) we have seen that with Nintex Workflow it is possible to look at how the workflows have run on a single item via the **view workflow history** option and the statistics via the **View statistics** option.

Nintex Workflow contains besides the per workflow history reports the options to use reports like usage, completed/ errored workflow, Overdue etc.

Nintex Reporting requires that the enterprise features solution (nintexworkflow20** enterprisefeatures.wsp) has been deployed. In addition the Site collection feature **Nintex Workflow Reporting Web Parts** and the site feature **Workflow Enterprise Reporting** need to be enabled.

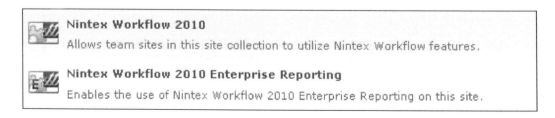

The Nintex Workflow reports can now be found via the Site Settings, under the section Nintex Workflow and then the last option View reports.

All reports are predefined and can be enabled or disabled from the SharePoint Central Administration; this is also the place to add new custom reports.
In the Nintex Workflow 2007.sdk there is a section about creating custom reports, this isn't in the 2010 sdk.

The following reports are by default available.
- Approver Performance Statistics
- Completed Workflows
- Errored Workflows
- 12 Month Usage Summary
- 30 Day Usage Summary
- 3 Month Usage Summary
- Workflow Performance
- Workflows By Site
- Workflow Actions
- Workflows In Progress
- Overdue Workflows.

Two cool reports are the Workflow Performance and the Approver Performance as this tells us how fast the workflows are executed and how the users respond to these workflows. The Errored Workflows report is a good indication to use for the quality of the created workflows. If the errored workflows are high this could indicate that the workflow designers requires more training.

If the expected duration in workflows are set the Overdue Workflows report will show these workflows.

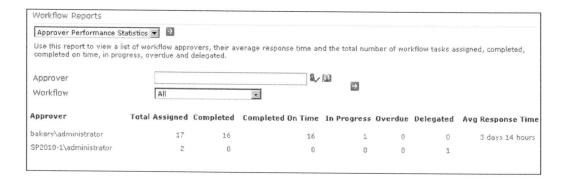

Nintex web parts

We have looked at the reporting options that are available in Nintex. Nintex also created web parts that can be used to display these reports in several different forms.

The following web parts are available from Nintex:

> **The User-based Workflow tracking web parts are available in Nintex Standard**

- My Workflow Tasks; display the tasks that are assigned to the current user.
- Workflows I've Started; this web part displays the workflow where the current user is the initiator
- Workflow Chart Viewer; create a workflow report in a chart view format
- Workflow Report Viewer; view a report in a grid based format.

If you want to use all the available web parts you will need to purchase the enterprise license for the **Chart Viewer** and **Report Viewer**. The User-based Workflow are in the standard license limited to the current site. For an overview on Site Collection or Farm wide you also need to have the enterprise license.

My Workflow Tasks

Using the two user workflows web parts is relatively simple if you have configured web parts in the past. Set the page in edit mode and add the web part on the page. Edit the web part to configure its properties.

You can choose the scope from where you want the data from; you would often choose for the Site Collection option on the front page of your site and per site on individual sites.

Also a point to note is the Item URL option, this is where you can select the destination where the link will point to.

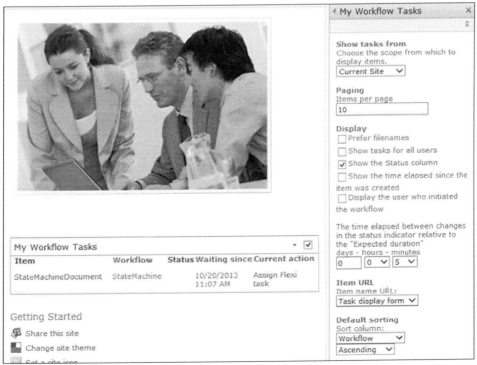

Editing the My Workflow Tasks webpart

Workflows I've started

The workflows I've started displays an overview of the status of the workflows you started.

As the same as with the previous web part you can also choose to get the workflow data from the Farm, Site Collection or Current site. If the scope is set to Farm it's best to set a reasonable item limit on the items per page otherwise the rendering of the page will be slowed down due to the heavy load.

In the beginning when you start to use these web part most users will want to see all workflows and their outcome (running, completed, errored and canceled). After a few months the users in most organizations want to view all workflows except the completed.

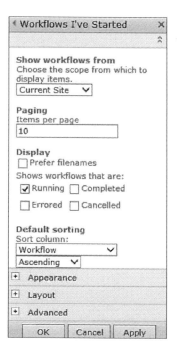

Report Viewer

With the report viewer web part you can select a report and show the result in this web part. As with the reports you here also have the option to filter the results and the option to limit the amount of results can be set.

When you set the Chrome type of the web part to the options **Default, Title** or **Title and Border** users can use the Export to Excel from the web part menu to export the result and modify if required.

The Workflow Report Viewer web part

Chart Viewer

The Chart viewer web part makes it possible to create chart views from the reports, the default or custom reports.

After the web part is added to the page and the report that needs to be displayed is selected from the **Chart to display** drop down list click on the **Configure display settings** to configure the chart.

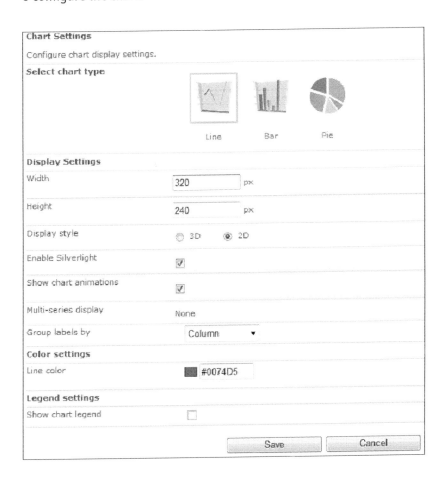

Editing the Chart Settings

When the option Enable Silverlight is checked, all users need to have Silverlight installed to be able to view the chart. Because Silverlight is stated to be End-of-Live by Microsoft it's recommended to leave this option disabled.

Chart Viewer web part

Modifying forms with InfoPath

The start and task forms that are used in Nintex Workflow can be changed if the SharePoint version is SharePoint enterprise and the client configuring the form has InfoPath 2010 installed. These forms can be modified:

- Start form
- Request approval
- Request review
- Request data
- Assign Flexi task.

Changing the start form

The start form can be changed in the overall Workflow Settings from the current workflow. The following options are available:

- Default form, not changeable by the users
- InfoPath form, the form can be adjusted with InfoPath
- Custom form, a developed form, contains a link to the startpage.

After setting the option to use InfoPath you can click the **Edit Start Form** button in the Workflow Settings menu to open **Edit with Microsoft InfoPath 2010**.

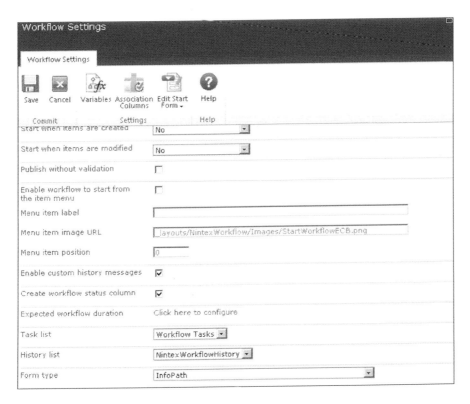

Setting the form type to InfoPath

In the following image we have created a custom start form for a Request for Change (RFC) process workflow. There are a few startdata variables defined that are displayed in this form. An image is added to personalise the form. The overview of the steps that the workflow are going to follow aren't available.

Custom Start form

Changing the approval form

Changing a workflow form can be done via the corresponding action. In the menu of the action is the option Edit Task Form; select this and from the menu click on the **Edit with Microsoft InfoPath 2010** option.

In the following image we have modified an Assign Flexi task with three outcomes:

- Approve
- Reject
- Request more information.

The options that can be changed in the approval form are limited as the actions that need to be executed are also limited.

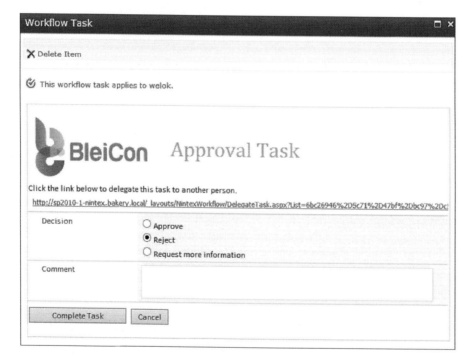

Custom Approval form

Changing the request data form

As we have seen with the other task-typed actions also the form of the request data action can be modified with InfoPath.

The Request data action form that we have created in the next image could be used if a task is escalated and more information is required from a user to continue the task.

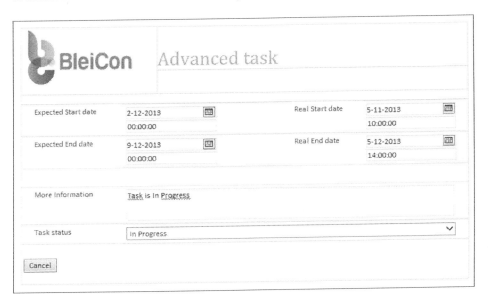

Custom request form

Data context

We have seen that when we used the insert reference option to add data to an action there were also data fields available that we didn't create but were part of the workflow or location. These fields can also be entered in a custom form.

Open the InfoPath form and choose from the top menu the section DATA, select the Show Fields option. The Fields are displayed at the right. Click on the **Show advanced view link**. Select from the data source (the pull down that displays Main) the secondary NWContext source. These fields can now be added to the form and extended the functionality of the form further.

Changing the data fields

If you want to change data in an InfoPath form using Nintex Workflow have a look at our blog at:

http://www.bleicon.nl/index.php/en/blog-en/item/1-update-infopath-form-with-nintex-workflow

Hands-on: Using the Nintex Live catalog

1. Go to the **Central Administration**, Nintex Workflow Management.
2. Select **Live Settings** and Click on **Enable**. Close with **OK**.
3. Go to the site collection features via **Site Actions**, **Site Settings**.
   You can find them beneath Site Collection Administration.
4. **Activate Nintex Workflow - Nintex Live catalog**.
5. Return to your library and the workflow settings, click **Manage Workflows** with Nintex Workflow.
6. Click on the **Create link** to create a new workflow.
7. Choose the **Blank Template**.
8. Click in the Top menu for the option **Catalog**.

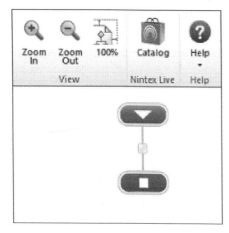

9. Click in the Filter by section under Category for the option **Social**.
10. Search for the action **Twitter Tweet**.
11. Click on the **Add** button next to the **Twitter Tweet**, this will change to Pending.
12. Click on **OK** so the action is added to the Nintex Action menu.

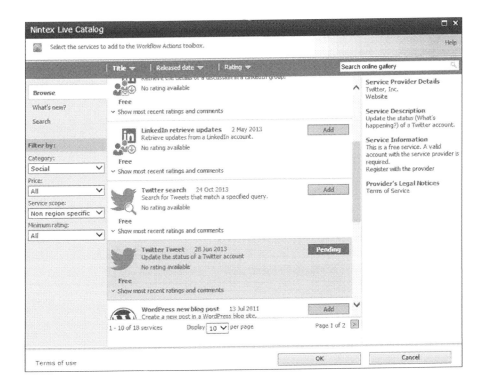

13. In the Action Menu there is a new menu item Nintex Live.
14. **Drag** the SharePoint create list item on the canvas.
15. View the requirement fields.

Hands-on: Using Twitter action

In the following hands-on we will use the just added Twitter Tweet action in a simple workflow. As the Twitter action requires a real account we assume that you have a Twitter account.

1. Create a custom list named **Twitter** with the following fields.
   a. **Title,** Single line of text. Limit the field to 140 characters.
2. Create a blank workflow to the list.
3. **Add** the Twitter Tweet action to the workflow.
4. **Add** your account to the **Authorizing user** field.
5. Set the **Tweet text** field to the current item **Title**.

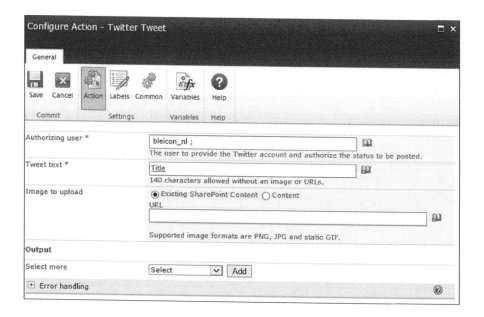

6. **Save** and **Publish** the workflow as TwitterWorkflow
7. Create a new item to the list and start the workflow
8. You will receive an e-mail requesting your approval to proceed

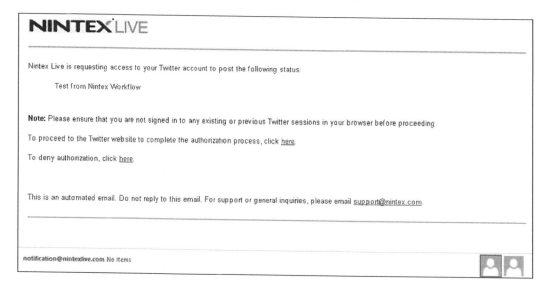

9. Click on authorize app to give Nintex Live the permission to act on your behalf.

10. You can choose to have the authorization be saved so you don't have to authorize Nintex Live again.

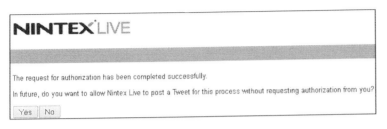

11. When you open Twitter you will see that Nintex has created the tweet

Advanced Hands-on: Twitter on time

You can also use the twitter action to send a twitter feed on a scheduled time:

*   Add a date and time field to the previous created Twitter list
*   Add the Pause for action that looks at the date and time field.

You need to allow Nintex to act on your behalf and save this to Nintex if you want to work with scheduled actions.

10 • Maintaining Nintex Workflow

Nintex workflow is an application that doesn't require much maintenance from a system administrator point of view. During the installation of Nintex Workflow the administrator has configured the environment and if this doesn't grow spectacular the amount of work is minimal.

Manage content databases

If a new web application is created this also requires the creation of a new content database for the storage of SharePoint content. When using Nintex Workflow intensive this is a good trigger to also create a Nintex Workflow content database.
Microsoft recommends keeping the content databases for SharePoint below the 200GB per database and we recommend the same for Nintex workflow.

Create database

In the Central administration go to Nintex Workflow Management and select **Database setup**. Click **Add** content database.
Add the Database Name and select the option to Grant **service account access** to the database. This ensures that required accounts have direct access to the database.

Manage database mapping

When the database is created it needs to be connected to the web application.
If no database is selected Nintex will automatically connect to a database based on how many site collections this database already contains.

Connect to the Central administration, go to Nintex Workflow Management and select **Database setup**. Click **Manage database mappings**.
Look at the SharePoint content database you want to connect from the left and select the Nintex database from the right.

Use this page to manage the workflow content database mappings. Settings apply to new site collection activations only.

I Like It   Tags & Notes

Note: These changes can take up to 15 minutes to take effect. Restarting IIS will force the changes to take effect immediately.

Map SharePoint content database to Nintex workflow content database.

SharePoint Content Database	Map to Workflow Content Database
SP_Content_Claim (SQL1\sp2010)	Any available workflow content database ▾
SP_Content_MySites (SQL1\sp2010)	Any available workflow content database ▾
SP_Content_Nintex (SQL1\sp2010)	Any available workflow content database ▾
SP_Content_Portal (SQL1\sp2010)	Any available workflow content database ▾

| OK | Cancel |

The mapping is displayed in the View database mappings if the site collection features are activated.

Archiving workflow data

Over time the Nintex Workflow databases will continue to grow with historical information about workflows that have been executed. SharePoint uses a daily Workflow Auto Cleanup job function to delete workflow instances and tasks that still exist after 60 days that the workflow is completed or canceled to reduce space. For more information see

http://technet.microsoft.com/en-us/library/ee662522%28v=office.14%29.aspx

There is the option to disable the automatic cleanup of workflow, but a better option is to archive the relevant information retrieved during the workflow. Some legal processes even require that the process that is followed and its outcome must be stored for several years. Organizations that have these requirements need to have a procedure for archiving.

Purging workflow data

By using the purging workflow data option there is the option to delete data from the Nintex Workflow database that has become obsolete. This may be needed for decreasing the size of the database, deleting test data or the workflow items and lists are deleted.

To purge workflow data follow the next steps:

- Go to the Central administration
- Select Nintex Workflow management and click on **Purge workflow data**
- Select the radio button next to the required option, and click on **Query**
- The results are returned to the page and can be deleted with the Purge option.

Purging data can also be done on site collection and site level.

Work with caution when using the purging option as data cannot be recovered without restoring the database via a restore procedure.

Manage workflow actions

Enable actions

During the installation we have enabled all workflow actions via the central administration. You can adjust the availability of actions by unselecting them or modifying the permission of that action.

An example: creating a workflow with a query SQL action is something an IT-pro or developer should know how to do. But does this mean that a normal user knows how he must create a query that retrieves the smallest amount of data, or know what the impact of a large query is on a SQL server? Probably not and preventing these users from using the Query SQL action is likely therefor a good reason.

Enforce allowed actions

With the option **Enforce allowed actions at run time** the workflow checks if all actions are allowed to be used by the current user. A workflow could be created by a designer that has permissions to all actions; the users that need to run the workflow aren't allowed to use some actions. The **Enforce allowed actions** at run time ensures that these users can't use these action.

If there are actions that aren't allowed the workflow will error. This prevents the use of unauthorized actions, default SharePoint functions aren't affected.

Custom actions

With the option **add Custom actions** the self-created actions can be uploaded and activated in Nintex.

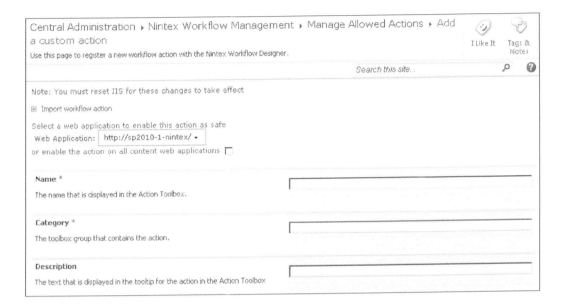

Import the .nwa file solution file via the Import workflow action.

After the import is completed the details from the nwa file are set and click on **OK** to save the custom solution. More information about creating a custom action can be found in the **Nintex Workflow 2010 SDK**.

Permissions

Working with permissions can go from easy to very complicated in Nintex Workflow in just a few steps.

Setting permissions on single items and actions, or preventing a function for a single user isn't advisable when looking for the maintainability of the system and preventing complexity. Yes, often enough customers want to give an entire department one type of permission except the trainees of that department. In that case always look at the lowest common denominator in groups, functions, and tasks to keep an overview; create new SharePoint or AD groups for these functions if required.

A permission design is recommended when the number of site collections and site permissions are growing.

Setting the permissions on site level can be done by a site and farm administrator, setting permissions on the web application requires of course farm administrator permissions.

Setting workflow permissions

Nintex Workflow uses the pre-build SharePoint permission to set the allowed Nintex permissions; this helps in keeping the complexity limited.

The permissions can be set on site collection or site level and use the Inherits to propagate the permissions to a lower level.

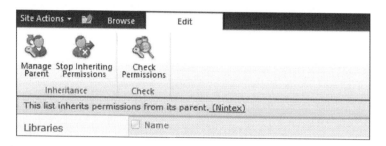

The users that are going to create and maintain workflows need access to the Workflow Designer. They therefore need to have the design permissions on the site where they are creating the workflows.

Users that are appointed as approvers or reviewers for the corresponding workflow actions need to have contribute permissions.

And those users that need to start workflows, add schedules, view history and progress reports also need to have contribute permissions

Set actions permissions

We have already looked at setting permissions on actions in the **Setup and Administration** section of this book. We used the example where we would limit the use of the **Execute SQL** action for non IT'pros.

In the Central administration we can use the page **Manage Allowed Action**s for permissions on all actions or for a single action.

Select a single action and click on the Edit permissions.

The checkbox **Make this action available to all users** sets the group NT AUTHORITY\ authenticated users in the Users/Groups field. This group represents all users that are authenticated, and as all users need to be authenticated this therefore means every user.

Set action permissions

Select Users

These users will have access to create workflows containing this action. Enter users separated by semi-colons.

Users/Groups:

NT AUTHORITY\authenticated users ;

☑ Make this action available to all users

OK   Cancel

Deselect the checkbox **Make this action available to all users** and select the active directory groups that require permissions to the action.

These settings can be modified on the site collection level or inherited.

In the previous part we have seen that we can use the **Enforce allowed actions** to be sure that the current initiator is allowed to run all actions in the current workflow.

Workflow constants permissions

The use of working with constants also introduces a potential security risk if these constants are used for storing credentials.

The risks of misusing a constant by users to execute tasks where they don't have permissions need to be prevented, otherwise users could, for example, create workflows that give their account permissions.

In the example below we have a constant with a SharePoint Farm administrator account in it; we select the constant and then click on **Edit permissions**.

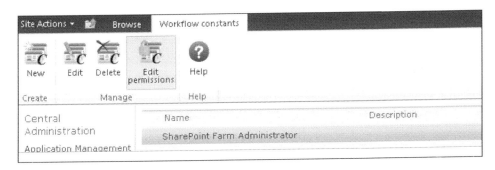

Set the Radio Button in the Permissions section to Server Farm administrators and remove the group **NT AUTHORITY\authenticated** users from the **Specific users** field.

On site level these permissions can also be changed except that the Farm administrators group here is the Team Site administrators group.

Best practices for constant security

The ultimate structure would be that for every task that requires credentials a unique service account would be created in AD or the LOB application. This account is then entered in a unique constant in Nintex workflow.

For every service account an Active Directory group is created that get permissions on the corresponding constant.

The users that are allowed to use the constants are added as members of the AD group.

11 • Where to go from here

Congratulations you have made it to the end: you have seen all the actions
and options you need to know on how to create a Nintex workflow. But what now?
How to do go further and get better workflows or what if your workflow breaks?
In this chapter we are looking at the thing you also need to know when becoming
a true Nintex workflow master.

Practise, practise and practise

Why is there in almost every language a saying that is something like:
"Practise makes perfect?" Because it is al so true.
We have created so many workflows that we stopped counting and with every workflow
that we created the overall quality of the workflows where getting better. So will your
workflows with practise, practise and practise.
Even the creation of a silly workflow that counts the days till you holiday will help in
this practise.
Look around your organisation at the processes that are used. Where can you add value
for your organisation by automating these processes?
There is one thing that you need to remember before you go berserk on workflow
creations and that's the ROI of the workflows. What is the Return on Investment(ROI)
with this workflow?

ROI of workflows

Because you are using workflows we can assume that you already want to automate business process so they are more efficient and therefore reducing the cost of IT, leaving more
money for growth or R&D (or golf). But when people start to create workflows they get
enthusiastic about the workflow creation and most of them get a "wish list" in there head
about the workflows they want to create. For a trainer it's great to work with eager and
devoted students but this wish list isn't always the list of the organisation.

You can create a wish list but ask yourself the following questions when creating that list:

- Which processes are the most time-consuming in our company?
- Where are the services to our users or customers suffering the most?
- Which processes do recur most frequently?
- Which are the most expensive processes for the company?
- Which process failures are visible to our customers?

This is just a list of questions you can ask yourself but you can image that this list could be different for your organisation where for example you want to reduce the possibility on human error options as much as possible.

The list that you created can be filtered further if you also check the process you want to automate against the following:

The time it takes the process manually, multiplied with how often the process is executed against the time it takes to create the workflow.

If an action takes 4 hours to complete and is executed 4 times a year this means that the action takes 16 hours a year. If the creation and the maintenance of the workflow is more than these 16 hours, this isn't a good candidate for a workflow.

A process that takes up only 1 hour, but occurs 5 times a week results in a process that takes up 250 hours a year. If the creation of a workflows to replace the manually steps costs 40 hours this is a great candidate for workflows automation.

An error! And now?

As with all software solutions that is being build sooner or later you may receive an error in the solution. This happens to everyone building a solution and isn't something to worry about; it is if you can't find the error.
We used a little bit of error handling in the chapter working with external sources where we forced the workflow to continue on error logging. Now we are going to look at where we can find the error.

Log in history list

When a workflow crashes with an error it is best to add extra logging to the workflow and see where the workflows errors in the process. With the Log in history list action you can write events to the Workflow History list to view after the workflow has been executed (and fails again). Variables are notorious for errors in workflows as they can contain unexpected data due to an incorrect query or a different variable type.

Add a Log in history list action direct after a variable is filled or used and configure this action to write the content of the variable. If the workflow contains many variables it is best to first set the name of the variable you are examine.

There is a maximum length of 255 characters in the history list entry.
Any additional text will be trimmed from the entry.
Also the results of a webservice query can be logged in the history list. Because of the character limitation it is best not to store the variable collection but all single results in the log.

Run now

There are actions that have the option to test the action while it is being configured.
The **Query list** and **Call web service** are best examples of the **Run now** option.

When an action is configured clicking the Run Now button will open a new screen where the results can be tested. As this screen displays in red: Pressing Execute means Execute! The action will be processed and this can mean that data is retrieved or a web service is triggered. Be careful what is being tested with this option therefore.

As the Run Now option only triggers the current action all data from other actions and variables are unaware in this action. If the action uses variables, they need to be converted to data before the Run Now can be used.

Disable

When a single action is responsible for the crash of a workflow it can be an option to disable that action temporarily and test the workflow first without this action.
An action can be easily disabled by selecting it from the configuration menu. After the disabling the action turns grey so users can easily identify the disabled actions.

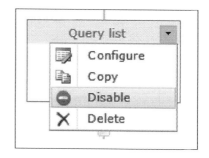

Workflow Error notification

If a workflow gets an error, the default option is to send a message to the initiator of the workflow, this is for testing perfect. If the workflow errors in a production environment, it isn't always advisable to send a notification to an initiator, this may result in more questions than answers for the initiator. And on scheduled workflows the initiator is a system account. For these two examples there is the option to specify other e-mail addresses to receive a notification on error. A shared team mailbox of an IT department can be used to receive these notifications.

Documentation

Because it is so easy to create a workflow we almost forget that we also need to document the created workflows, and this is defiantly true if you aren't maintaining the workflows.

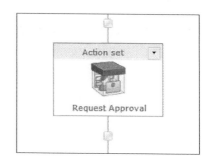

Writing down how your workflow is build up and how variables are used can help enormous when you need to fix a crashing workflow that you have created a half year ago. And the documentation doesn't have to be that complicated; for a workflow with a few actions a workflow description and setting labels can be enough. For larger workflows, workflow that are nested or workflows that retrieve data from other systems it is advisable to create a design document.

Set Title & Description

Setting an obvious title for a workflow is something that everybody understands but the option underneath the set a title, the description isn't always used. This field is as important as the title field and must contain descend information about the workflow. What does the workflow do in overview, what are the start-up options and how is the interaction if required?
Setting a correct and informative description saves the time required to open a workflow to see how it is configured.

> Tip: the change comments is there also for a reason!

Set labels

One of the first thing that we wrote about when using actions is that you can set the labels of an action. This is a very easy method to describe the variable that is used in the action or the calculation that is used.
When you use action sets it is best to set the label of the action set to the process you are executing in the action set.

Design document

Workflow that are more complex require more documentation than possible in the description or labelling; for these workflows we often use a design document. In a design document you provide information about the goal of the workflow, the requirements and many more. In the appendix we have added a Workflow design template you can use for the documentation of your own workflows.

12 • Actions

With so many actions it's easy to get lost in all the options you have at your disposal.
In this chapter we are going to describe in detail the actions that are available.
As Nintex workflow matures, the actions that are available for Nintex workflow
are going to increase, especially with the introduction of Nintex Live.
To give a structure to the list with actions, the actions in this chapter are divided in
the groups as they are available in Actions menu. There is no distinction on standard or
enterprise actions, the description of the action tells if an enterprise license is required.
We start with the most used and shortest section: Commonly used

Commonly used

Send notification

License type: Standard

Sends a notification to the user defined in the To field, this can be a handpicked user
or a dynamic selected user. The notification doesn't have to be an e-mail message,
if the organization has sms configured this can also be used as notification.

Assign Flexi task

License type: Standard

Sets a task to a user or group. The outcome can be adjusted for different outcomes,
where the default values are Approve and Reject. The action contains Reminders
and Escalation options.

Set a condition **License type: Standard**

Conditions are used to have a choice in your workflow; if the selected field is set to this value then follow this path otherwise follow this path. For more information see the "Creating advanced workflows" section.

Integration

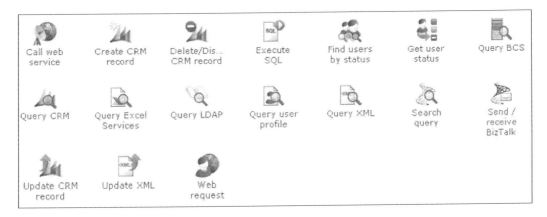

Call web service **License type: Standard**

Used for retrieving SOAP messages via web services. As SharePoint also uses web services this action can be used to retrieve data from the current but also a different SharePoint environment. For more information see the chapter "Working with External sources".

Create, Delete, update and Query CRM **License type: Enterprise**

These actions are created for working with Microsoft Navision CRM v4.0 and v5.0.
The Nintex workflow Enterprise license is required for these actions.

Execute SQL **License type: Enterprise**

Used for executing SQL command against databases.
For more information see the chapter "Working with External sources".

Find user by and get user status

License type: Enterprise

Actions used for connecting to Microsoft Lync. The Find user by status could be used to get the available user from Lync and set that person as approver for an item.

Query BCS

License type: Enterprise

The Query BCS action can be used for interacting with the Business Connectivity Service of SharePoint. This SharePoint enterprise feature makes it possible to connect to external LOB applications via a generic interface. For more information see the chapter "Working with External sources".

Query Excel Services

License type: Enterprise

Also a SharePoint enterprise function: Excel Services. Excel Services can be used to let users that don't have Excel locally installed use Excel and let SharePoint calculate Excel workbooks. In the Excel Services action you can retrieve data from this Excel Services and use it in a workflow.

Query LDAP

License type: Enterprise

LDAP stands for Lightweight Directory Access Protocol and is used for directory services as Active Directory. The action can be used to get information such as who is in a group or which groups is that user member of.

Query user

License type: Enterprise

The user profile services (UPS) is used for creating a synchronization connection between Active Directory and SharePoint. The UPS is the location where account information is stored, via the Query user profile action this info can be retrieved.

Query and update XML

License type: Enterprise

The results from a web service response, an InfoPath form, communication with BizTalk, there is a lot of data in Nintex workflows that is based on XML data. With these 2 actions you can get XML information and modify it.

Search query

The Search Query is an action that is used to check the search results from SharePoint. If you don't want items to appear in the search results, for example the administrator password, you can create a workflow that checks this and sends a message as the results appear.

Send / receive BizTalk

BizTalk is a Microsoft application used for the automation business processes via enterprise application integration structure. This action is used for communicating with the BizTalk environment and processing the result back in the current workflow.

Web request

Where the Call web service is used for the query of a web service, web request performs a HTTP request to a URL. It can be used to perform a variety of HTTP operations.

Libraries and lists

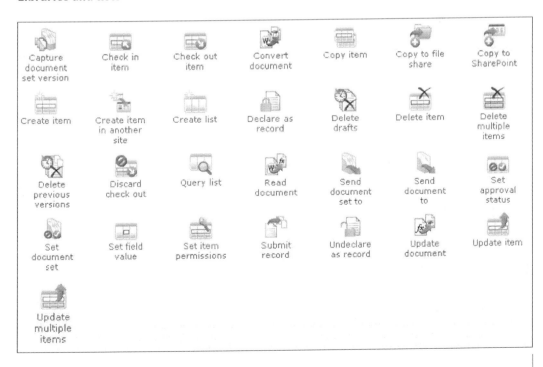

Capture document set version	Check in item	Check out item	Convert document	Copy item	Copy to file share	Copy to SharePoint
Create item	Create item in another site	Create list	Declare as record	Delete drafts	Delete item	Delete multiple items
Delete previous versions	Discard check out	Query list	Read document	Send document set to	Send document to	Set approval status
Set document set	Set field value	Set item permissions	Submit record	Undeclare as record	Update document	Update item
Update multiple items						

Capture document set version /
Send document set to repository /
Set document Set

License type: Standard

These workflow actions are for working with document sets. To use document set, first activate the site collection feature "Document Sets", then set the document library to allow management of content types. Finally, add the document set content type to the library. The send document set to repository also requires that the "Content Organizer" SharePoint site feature is enabled in the SharePoint site.

Check in / out item

License type: Standard

Check an item in or out. For example if a checked out document isn't modified for a week it is checked in so other users have the possibility to modify it.

Convert document

License type: Enterprise

Convert the current document or the document at a giving URL to another file type. Word documents and templates, PDF, rtf or XML are outcomes of the conversion.

This action requires the Word automation services to be configured in the SharePoint farm and needs the SharePoint server version of SharePoint. This is not available in the Share-Point Foundation edition.

Copy item

License type: Standard

This action makes it possible to copy the current item to another list, or another item from one list to another list. It's possible to override the item if it already exists.
This action uses a batch type job queue and may not execute all changes directly.

Copy to file share / SharePoint

License type: Standard

Copy the current item to a network file share or another SharePoint environment.
This action for SharePoint contains a few options for duplicate items,
you can copy the folder structure and also the metadata.
The username and password can be provided as well as error handling.

Create item

Create a list item in one of the current sites lists or libraries. The new item ID can be saved in a variable.

This action uses a batch type job queue and may not execute al changes directly.

Create item in another site

Add an item to a list or library in another SharePoint site in the current farm. All the data fields can be filled with variables, the new item ID can be saved in a variable.

Create list

Create a list or library in the current or a selected site. The action uses the list template overview for specifying the required list/ library.

This action can be used for example to create a library for every customer via a workflow.

Query List

The query list action is used to retrieve data from lists or libraries into workflow variables. The query can be configured via a Query builder or via a CAML editor. To retrieve data from outside the current site the CAML editor is required.

The variable type to store the outcome it can be a collection or a single item depending on the query.

Read document / Update document

This workflow actions can be used to retrieve and update values from a "content control" within a Word document and store the value in a workflow variable.

These actions require SharePoint Server and Nintex Enterprise. The Word document also needs to be an docx type document and have content control defined.

Send document to repository

A workflow action to send the current document to a repository or records center.
To be able to set rules and send documents, the "Content Organizer" SharePoint site feature has to be enabled in the SharePoint site.

Set approval status

Action to set the approval status of the current item and the option for a comment.
If the library is configured with the content approval option the documents in that library that are not approved are not visible for everyone.
Mostly used with the Assign Flexi task action.

Set field value / Update item

Set field value is used for updating a field in the current item, the update item makes it possible to update an item in the current site.

Update multiple items

Workflow action that is used to update several items from one list at once.
The action contains a filter to select which items need to be updated.
This action could be used to set the status of multiple items if a phase is reached.

Set item permissions

The permissions of this item or another item in the same list/ library can be modified. You can set unique permissions or inherit them from the parent.

Setting item level permissions is normally a big no-go in SharePoint because of the complexity that you are introducing. When you set these permissions via a workflow you can reduce the complexity because of the repetitive steps.

These two workflow actions will submit an undeclared current item that the workflow is running on to the SharePoint Records Center.

This action requires SharePoint Server and Nintex Enterprise.

Logic and flow

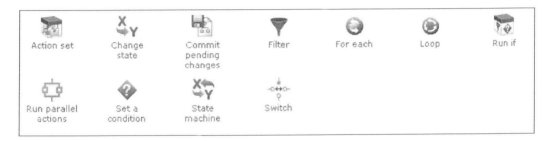

Action set   **License type: Standard**

The Action set action is used for structuring your workflow by grouping actions together. Action sets can also be saved as snippets. For more information see the chapter "Creating advanced workflows".

Change state / State machine   **License type: Standard**

For the State machine workflows actions have a look at the chapter "Almost programming".

Commit pending changes   **License type: Standard**

This action is used to be sure that all changes that are pending are committed.

If you use many batched type actions, like create or copy item, this action ensures that these batches are committed.

Filter

This workflow action ends the workflow if a configured condition is not met, the configuration of this action is similar to the Set a condition action.

For each

The For each action is used to loop through the values in a collection variable. You can add child actions that also need to be executed when processing the collection.

Loop

This action looks the same as the For each action except that this action only stops when a statement reaches a falls status.

Run if

The Run if action looks like the action set action on a box but the function is totally different. If the Run if statement is true the actions in the Run if box are executed, otherwise they are skipped.

This action is often used when a simple step in the workflow needs to be in- or excluded.

Run parallel action

Can be used to run several actions at once. This action was used in the earlier versions of Nintex to run on one site the approval request and on the other site the task reminder. This use is now redundant as it is packed in approval request item itself.

When you set the parallel action be sure that these actions have a relation and that one isn't slowing the process for the other down.

Set a condition

See the Set a condition underneath the Commonly used section.

This workflow action directs the flow of actions based on the value of a single variable. A branch for each possible defined value is used to determine which branch of workflow actions will run. This action looks like the "State Machine workflow functionality", except that this action switches only once.

Nintex Live

As Nintex Live is building up and evolving it is difficult to describe the actions that are available. Therefor we have chosen to describe the categories:

- *Communication*

Contains actions that are associated with communication, as e-mail and SMS actions. The StrikeIron e-mail verification and SMS alerts and notification are actions that can be used.

- *Converters & tools*

The converters & tools section contains the most actions after the SharePoint section. With Converters is meant actions that allows for changing the input of data like Google and Bitly URL Shortener or Bing Text to speech and Bing translation. The Tools section contains a few IT tools like the creation of virtual cloud servers on Amazon EC2 or Rackspace. The other tools are mostly for cloud storage interactions with Box, DropBox, Google Drive and SkyDrive.

- *Finance*

In the Finance section the actions that interact with finance values are stored. This section contains the StrikeIron exchange rate and currency converter.

- *Reference*

The Reference section is used for actions that retrieve their data from other locations and use therefore a reference. The news and weather forecast are examples of these type of references.

- *SharePoint*

This section contains all actions that have an interaction with Office 365, not only the SharePoint part of Office 365 as you might expect from the name but also the management There are actions to work with items and documents as well as actions for managing users and licenses.

- *Social*

Social section contains the actions from the most well-known social networks: Facebook, LinkedIn and Yammer.

Operations

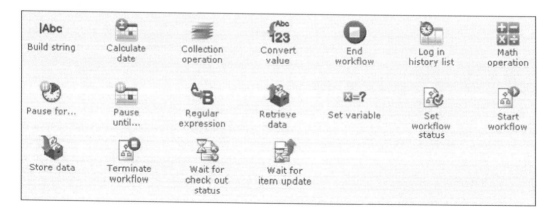

Build string

This action is used to reconfigure workflow data. You can use inline functions or add static data to dynamic data. An example is to get a value and turn this into a URL a reuse this in another action.

Calculate date

This workflow action allows a time period to be added or subtracted from a date
to create a new date. The outcome can be stored in a date/time variable or
in an ISO 8601 text variable.

Collection operation

This action provides direct access to the values in a collection variable. With this action
the collection can be altered, added, removed, counted or joined together.

Convert value

Convert a text variable in another variable type for future use in the workflow.
With the Culture option the Locale site culture can be modified, for example
the de-DE culture for Germany can be changed in nl-NL for the Netherlands.

End workflow / Start workflow / Terminate workflow

The terminate workflow stops all other workflow in the current site, where the start
workflow lets you start a workflow from the current site. The end workflow action stops
the current workflow.

Set workflow status

Set the status of a workflow (e.g. In Progress, Cancelled, Completed, Errored)
of the current item.

Log in history list

The log in the history list is used for writing data to the workflow history, this way the data
in a variable can be checked during a development phase.

Math operation

License type: Standard

This action allows the workflow to perform basic calculations at runtime for use within other actions in the workflow.

Pause for / pause until

License type: Standard

Pause the workflow for a specific period or until a specific period. As Nintex workflow works with the SharePoint timer services these pauses aren't minute specific.

Regular expression

License type: Standard

This workflow action allows a regular expression to be performed on a block of text. A regular expression is a pattern that can match various text strings. It can be used to either check if the text matches a regular expression pattern or replace parts of the text that match a regular expression with different text.

Retrieve data / Store data

License type: Standard

These workflow actions can be used to store data between workflow instances (running workflows).

Set variable

License type: Standard

This action sets a value in a variable for use in the workflow via lookup.

Wait for check out status

License type: Standard

This action will let the workflow wait until the check-out status changes to the required status.

Wait for item update

License type: Standard

The action will hold the workflow until a field in the current item is updated to a prefilled value.

Provisioning

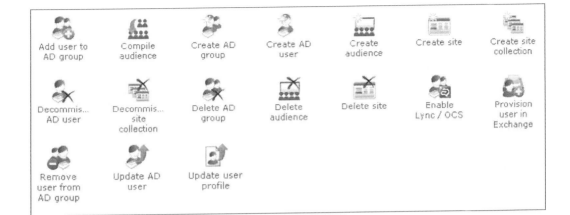

Add user to AD group • Compile audience • Create AD group • Create AD user • Create audience • Create site • Create site collection

Decommis... AD user • Decommis... site collection • Delete AD group • Delete audience • Delete site • Enable Lync / OCS • Provision user in Exchange

Remove user from AD group • Update AD user • Update user profile

---

Add / Remove user from AD Group   **License type: Enterprise**

This action uses LDAP to add or remove a user from or to a specific AD group.

Create / compile / delete audiences   **License type: Enterprise**

These workflow actions are used for the creation or deletion of audiences.
Audiences are groups of users that can be used to target content on a website.
After the creation of the audiences the action compile audiences needs to run to enable
the audience.

Create / Delete AD Group   **License type: Enterprise**

This action uses LDAP that create or delete an AD group. You can set the group scope
and group type. This action is mostly used to automatic create an AD group when a site
is created and give this group permissions on the site.

Create / Decommision AD user   **License type: Enterprise**

These actions allow the creation or disabling of an AD user via LDAP. sAMAccountName
and Common name are required at creation. A password can be created and stored in
a workflow variable.

Create / Delete Site

License type: Enterprise

The names of these two actions already explain it, these are used to create or delete a site. There are a much options to select when creating a site.
The permissions to create or delete the site can as with most action be modified.

Create / Decommission Site collection

License type: Standard

Makes it possible to create or decommission a site collection, the web application and the primary administrator are required. There is no option to create host named site collection as these need to be created via PowerShell.

Enable Lync / OCS

License type: Enterprise

This action will enable OCS/LCS or Lync 2010 for an existing Active Directory user account.

Provision user in exchange

License type: Enterprise

The Provision User in Exchange workflow action will provision a mailbox for an Active Directory user account in the specified mailbox container or mailbox database location.

Update user profile

License type: Enterprise

This workflow action will update the SharePoint user profile service fields of a selected user. The action requires SharePoint server and Nintex Workflow Enterprise.

User interaction

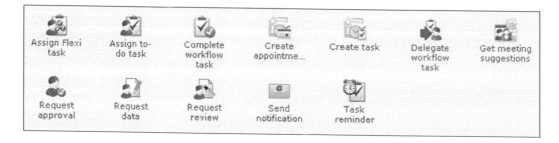

Assign Flexi task

See the Assign Flexi task in the section Commonly used.

Assign to-do task

This workflow action will assign a task to one or more users to complete.
The task is based on a Content type.

Complete workflow task

This action is the same function as the escalation complete task option in the
Assign Flexi task.

Create appointment

This workflow action creates a calendar appointment or meeting request in Microsoft
Exchange. The action contains a recurrence option from none till yearly.

Create task

This action is the same function as the escalation delegate task option in
the Assign Flexi task.

Delegate workflow task

Actions used for connecting to Microsoft Lync. The Find user by status could be used to get
the available user from Lync and set that person as approver for an item.

Get meeting suggestions

This workflow action will retrieve a series of meeting time suggestions based on a
specified criteria.

Request approval

License type: Standard

This action allows the request of one or more users to process an approval as part
of the workflow and is the simpler version of the Assign Flexi task action.

Request data

License type: Standard

This workflow action assigns a task to a specified user. To complete the task, the user
must provide a value for each data item specified in the action configuration.
The workflow will wait for the task to be completed before continuing the execution.
Once the task is completed, the data that the user entered is available within the workflow.

Request review

License type: Standard

This action is used to assign a task and send a notification to one or more users to review
an item as part of the workflow.

Send notification

License type: Standard

See the Send notification task in the section Commonly used.

Task reminder

License type: Standard

This action is an outdated action that was used to set task reminders outside
the approval action.

Appendix

Workflow design template

This template can be used for the documentation of your workflows.

Goal

Describe the purpose of the workflow. What is automated with this workflow and why is it necessary to automate the routine.

Requirements

Provide the requirements that are needed for this workflow

ID	Requirement	
RE01	example:	A Constant for a service account username and password needs to be created.
RE02	example:	The workflow needs to be executed every day.
RE03	example:	
RE04	example:	

Current situation

Describe the current situation that is going to be changed by the workflow. What are the current steps that need to be processed, either manual or already automated?

Feature situation

Describe the feature situation, what are the steps going to be in that situation. Is there still a manual interaction required or is there a dependence created with another application.

Flow

Create a visual representation of the workflow, this can also be a screenshot

Process

Describe the process that will be created.

Describe that startup option of the workflow (scheduled / on change / manual).

Describe when a user or group needs to provide manual interaction with the workflow.

If necessary create visual representation of this process.

Details of the workflow

Describe the details of the workflow

- Why are actions used
- Are there startup variables or constants used
- If data is retrieved provide information
- Error logging and error capturing
- Output.

Feature extensions

If there are improvement or bottlenecks that need to be addressed in feature releases they can be described. For example an interaction with a system that with this current release isn't available.

Used data and information

Provide an overview of the data and information that is used or modified in the workflow. This can be:

- SharePoint list items
- AD users and groups
- SQL data
- File locations.

Attachments

This space can be used for storing the commands that are used in the workflow.

Notes

Notes

Notes

Notes

Printed in Great Britain
by Amazon.co.uk, Ltd.,
Marston Gate.